The Complete Book of
Inflatable Boats

The Complete Book of Inflatable Boats

This publication is designed to acquaint the reader with inflatable boats and boating, and is not intended to be a primer in the basics of operation in the marine environment. Readers who are inexperienced, or who have limited experience, are strongly urged to seek instruction in boating safety and handling from other sources before venturing out on the water.

The information contained in this book is based on the usual practices and procedures commonly used by inflatable boat owners throughout the world, and is reported in this sense. The reader must always defer to the limitations of the law, his own experience, current operating conditions, and the exercise of good judgment when operating a boat.

The Author and Publisher both specifically disclaim any personal liability for loss or risk which might occur, either directly or indirectly, from the reader's interpretation of the information which is contained herein.

The Complete Book of

Inflatable Boats

By
CDR Don Hubbard, USN (Ret)

Western Marine Enterprises, Inc.
Box Q, Ventura, California 93002

By the Same Author:
Ships-In-Bottles

©1980 by Don Hubbard

Library of Congress Cataloging in Publication Data

Hubbard, Donald, 1926-
The complete book of inflatable boats.
1. Inflatable boats. I. Title. II. Title: Inflatable boats.
VM360.H8   623.8'202   79-27460
ISBN 0-930030-15-X

Book Design: Fred Colcer

PUBLISHED BY WESTERN MARINE ENTERPRISES, INC.
Publishers of the *Pacific Boating Alamanac*
and other marine books. Catalog on request.
Box Q, Ventura, California 93002

In Canada:
Gordon Soules Book Publishers
525-355 Burrard Street
Vancouver, B.C. V6C 2G8

*To all of my customers, through the years,
who came into my store to buy "rubber rafts",
and left with "inflatable boats".*

Don Hubbard

Contents

when inflating — Transporting the boat — Cartopping — Trailering — The use of launching wheels — Disassembly — Folding techniques — Storing the boat — Routine maintenance — Hull repairs — Cleanliness — Surface preparation — Sizing the patch — Patching cement — Acetone and toluene — Use of power tools — Applying the patch — Special repair techniques — Inside and outside patches — Repairing long rips — Repairing leaks on a seam — Reattaching wooden parts to the hull — Replacing the doublers — Reinforcing the transom — Cleaning the hull — Tar and grease — Rust stains — Marine growth — Surface coatings — Painting the hull — Mounting registration numbers — Avoiding theft

Loading the boat — Seating — Rowing the boat — Operating under power — Planing — High speed operations in rough seas — High speed turns — Anchoring — Towing an inflatable — Dinghies and tenders — Advantages — Storing on board — CO_2 emergency inflation devices — Converting your dinghy into a life boat — Some other hints for yachtsmen — Launching and recovery in surf — Handling trouble on the water — Righting an overturned boat — Scuba diving techniques — Waterskiing — Sailing — Fishing — Hunting — River-running — Rescue boats — Liferafts

U.S. Coast Guard required equipment — Signaling equipment — First aid equipment — General boating equipment — Bait tanks — Bathing ladders — Boat covers — Bow dodgers — Bow storage devices — Depth finders — Doelfin — Dry storage — Flags and flagstaffs — Floor coverings — Flexible fuel tanks — Launching wheels — Sailing equipment — Scuba tank racks — Seating devices — Self-bailing devices — Sun canopies — Windscreens

Part I: Dinghies, Kayaks and Canoes, Sportboats, Riverboats and Hybrids — Achilles — Avon — Barakuda — Bombard — Bonair — Boston Whaler — Callegari — Campways — Dyer — Explorer Boats — Hutchinson — Maravia — Metzeler — Northwest River Supplies — Novurania — Pyrawa — Rogue Inflatables — Rubber Crafters — Semperit — Sevylor — Zodiac

Part II: Liferafts
Avon — Givens — RFD-Patten — Sea-Jay Elliot YFC — Switlick — Winslow — Zodiac

APPENDICES

Acknowledgments:

I would like to acknowledge and give my most sincere thanks to the following individuals and companies whose contributions made this book possible:

Tom Norreys, Managing Director, Avon Inflatables Limited, who long ago encouraged this book and generously supplied me with much hard to find reference material from England and Europe; his associates, Andrew Dossett, Jerry Sehi, and Dave Geofferoy of Seagull Marine; Helmut Peters and his sons Andy and Mike of the Inflatable Boat Center (Metzeler); Konstantine Klimenko of Sevylor Inflatables; Burks Smith of Bonair Boats; Tim Curtis and Donna M. Smith of Zodiac of North America; Arthur D. Sams and Denice L. Wolfe of Proko International (Novurania Boats); Donn O. Morton of Port-A-Marine for his early help; Jay Murdock and Don Whorley of Ocean Ventures; Robert E. Marlowe of Port City Marine (Hutchinson Boats); Richard F. Ford of Maravia Corporation; Jon Osgood and Steve Horne of Campways; Jeff Qvale of British Motor Car Distributors (Callegari Boats); Steve Elliot of Elco Marine Sales (Baracuda Boats); Sonny Panzarella of Achilles Boats; Dick Fitzgerald of Discovery Boats; Jim Givens of Givens Buoy Rafts; Don Muldoon of San Diego Marine Exchange; Boston Whaler, Inc.; Northwest River Supplies; Leisure Imports (Pyrawa); Rogue Inflatables, Inc.; Rubber Crafters of West Virginia, Inc.; Steyr Daimler Puch of America (Semperit Boats); RFD-Patten, Inc.; The C.J. Hendry Company; The Winslow Company; Boat and Motor Sales (Zodiac West); The United States Navy Special Warfare Group; The American Boat and Yacht Council, Inc.; Boating Industries Association; The Royal National Lifeboat Institution; and the very cheerful and helpful staff of the Coronado Public Library.

In addition I would like to offer my very special thanks to the following people who, in varying degrees, lived through this thing with me and helped pull it off:

My valued business associate David J. Eberhardt who was the source of much knowledge, and our mutual friend, Doug Nelson; Commander Dallas B. Boggs, USN, and Commander Robert L. Dale, USN (Ret), both longtime friends; Paige Giberson, Sep Armstrong and Clay Cole who were fun to be around; and my three children, Leslie, Chris and Lauren, who each contributed in his own way and who made the whole effort worthwhile.

DON HUBBARD
Coronado, California

Introduction

In the last decade a mini-revolution in small boating has taken place in America. The inflatable boat has come of age, and it is no longer an unusual sight around marinas and launching ramps to see bags being unloaded from storage lockers or car trunks, and air being added to inflate a fabric hull. Onlookers still gather round — watching people work is the great American pastime — but inflatable boats have now been accepted, and even curious bystanders now appreciate that they are looking at real boats, rather than substitutes for real boats.

Good inflatables *are* real boats, and they are overwhelmingly practical and efficient boats as well. The little "rubber rafts", which appeared in surplus houses and discount stores after World War II, have evolved into truly sophisticated craft capable of filling any boating need. Whatever the requirement, whether it be water-skiing, river-running, canoeing or kayaking, Scuba diving, sailing, yacht tending, or landing Marines, there is an inflatable boat on the market today that can do the job as well, and often better, than any comparable hard boat.

Because the American public has begun to realize and accept this fact, inflatable sales have become the most rapidly growing segment of the small boating industry in the country today. In the last few years it has become a common occurrence for demand to exceed supply during the boating season, despite rising prices, stepped up production, and increasing numbers of importers and domestic manufacturers.

Despite this growing interest in inflatable boats, the American public has been given very little in the way of practical information about them. Articles, which have appeared from time to time in most major boating and outdoor magazines, have been informative, but they have also been incomplete, sometimes biased, and often inaccurate. Concurrently, the marine retail industry, which should be the normal source of information, has been extremely slow to respond. Marine sales personnel are often less informed than their customers. Too frequently their only response to questions about the boats is to hand the customer a manufacturers catalog to let him interpret the data for himself. To my mind this sales technique is hardly sufficient in a business where a buyer can be expected to put down hundreds, and often thousands, of dollars for a product that may appear to him to be little more than a sophisticated inner tube made of fabric, cement and wood.

Fortunately, a large part of the momentum in sales has occurred because the boats are their own best salesmen. Often a new owner will have purchased an inflatable simply because of its compactness and stowability. Not until later does he discover all of the additional benefits that the boats deliver. Benefits like super-stability, enormous payload capacity, versatility, economy of operation, extremely low maintenance, and long-term durability. These discovered qualities make inflatable owners an enthusiastic lot, and few street corner preachers are more vocal in a cause. The new owner tends to think of himself as a pioneer in a new type of boating, and he feels that he has gambled and won. No wonder then that inflatable owners do not hesitate to tell their story to any and all who are willing to listen. Naturally, this type of enthusiasm generates new customers, and in my own store, which specialized in inflatable craft, it was not unusual for a buyer to walk in and tell me exactly what boat and motor he wanted to buy, without prior discussion. When asked, it would often turn out that his selection had been made solely on the basis of a conversation with some enthusiastic owner. At the same time it was interesting to see that many of these new buyers were completely surprised when faced with the many other makes and models of inflatables on display.

Doubtless, for every individual who has learned about infla-tables by chance encounter there are many more who would be potential buyers if sufficient information were available to con-vince them about the boats.

That is one reason this book was written. It gives the American public a solid basis for comparing the inflatable to the hard boat, and it provides guidance in selection, use and care. There are sec-tions which discuss the characteristics, design and construction of the various types and styles of inflatables. There is a chapter on accessories, and there are chapters which speak about maintenance and repair, and about specific techniques for using the boats in a variety of applications. In short this book was designed to answer virtually any question that a potential buyer, current owner, or even a marine salesman, might want to ask about inflatable boats and boating.

There is a second reason for this book. Regrettably, whenever a newly introduced product is successful, there are those who are quick to exploit the advantage by selling poor quality merchandise at discount prices. This is especially true where you find a relatively uninformed public that is eager to buy, and a product that is relatively expensive. This describes the inflatable boat business in every respect, so it is not surprising that the lower priced "bargains" have already made their appearance. It is most unfortunate that these poorly made boats are not just limited to the discount stores. Some usually reliable outlets have also begun to feature this merchandise, probably because their buyers are no better informed about inflatables than the rest of the American public. Nevertheless, until this situation changes, the customer is best advised to educate himself. When there are enough informed buyers demanding quality boats, the reputable dealer will quickly upgrade his lines.

It is my hope that this book will help to generate these changes, at the same time that it stimulates the sale of these amazingly versatile small craft.

Chapter 1

The Inflatable Boat Comes of Age

There is an old saying that there are no footprints on the water, and without a doubt this is one of the major reasons why pleasure boating enjoys the tremendous popularity that it does today. The waters of our lakes, rivers, bays and oceans leave little record of the passage of man, and each weekend sailor can blaze his own adventurous pathway across this ever changing medium. The water offers the opportunity to get away from it all, without having to look at the inevitable piles of beer cans and trash, and with but few restrictions on freedom of movement. It offers the opportunity to take a thrilling ride on water-skis, or the chance to seek out some secluded gunk hole where the big ones are biting. For some it means drifting down a scenic river, and for others it means pitting their skill against the wind in a sailboat. Boating satisfies some primitive urge in man for adventure and excitement — the need to be outdoors and challenge the elements. It is this wide range of human interests and needs which every year lures hundreds of thousands of new participants into boating, and which keeps

The first manufactured Zodiac inflatable boat. Created in France in 1936 by Pierre Debroutelle. (Zodiac of North America)

the many, many millions of already hooked individuals coming back for more.

Yet boat ownership can have its problems. There are expenses involved — the cost of the boat and its accessories, and of fuel and upkeep. There are problems of transportation and storage, and there are the inevitable compromises between what one would like and what one can afford and use.

Difficult and conflicting demands always arise when considering the purchase of a new craft. Larger boats, which can accomodate the entire family or a number of friends, invariably means greatly increased ownership costs, while less expensive small craft restrict the number of passengers and are usually less versatile. Storage problems complicate the matter for the apartment and condominium dweller, while transporting a boat is often difficult for owners of motor homes and house trailers. This is also true for the increasing number of people who drive small sub-compact cars. Even

16

fuel prices have become a significant factor in small craft sales. The high-speed enthusiast, the water-skier, and the scuba diver, who all need large gas-gulping engines, are finding that escalating costs of foreign oil have caused a sharp rise in their recreational expenses. Some new boat purchases must be deferred because of this, and existing boats are used less often.

There is no single cure for all of these problems, but more and more people are finding that there is one type of small boat which can greatly minimize them. That boat is the modern inflatable.

The most immediate proof of this can be found in Europe. Inflatables were developed and refined there, and without question, Europeans are the world's most avid inflatable users. Some eighty percent of all their small craft purchases are of air-filled fabric boats, and it is not difficult to see why. Europeans do not have large garages, or yards, or driveways for storing hard boats. Most of their vehicles are smaller cars of limited horsepower, which are unsuitable for car-topping or pulling a trailer. Prepared launching ramps are not widespread, and extremely high costs for fuel have been a way of life to Europeans for many years.

What has all this got to do with inflatables? Just about everything. Inflatables fold down into small, lightweight packages, which takes care of the storage problem. They can be carried in the trunk or back seat of almost any automobile, which eliminates the need for trailers. Inflatables can be launched almost anywhere, which eliminates the need for ramps or other boat launching facilities. And because they are both lightweight and buoyant they can perform just as well as any hard boat, but with a much smaller and more economical engine.

Those are the more obvious features, but there are other plus factors as well. Any inflatable can safely carry a payload which is twice that of a comparable hard boat. This is because of the tremendous buoyancy of the pontoons, and these same pontoons impart an almost unbelievable stability to inflatable craft, to the point where they are almost impossible to capsize, even with the entire passenger load seated on one side.

17

A 12½-foot inflatable boat and motor fit nicely in the trunk of this car. Despite its size this boat can easily carry its 1250 pound rated capacity. (Avon Inflatables Limited)

Maintenance costs are at an absolute minimum because the fabric parts of the boat require little more than an occasional hosing down or a periodic scrubbing. With the exception of a small amount of woodwork on some boats, there is no requirement for sanding and scraping, varnishing or painting.

Inflatable hulls are resilient — they bounce off when they impact against a hard object — and for this reason they are far less susceptible to damage than rigid hull boats of wood, metal or fiberglass.

Perhaps most importantly, good inflatables are unparalleled for safety. Even when full of water they will float high enough to permit the engine to run, and if the hull is punctured there is only inconvenience, rather than danger, because the inflated tubes are separated into a number of individually independent sections. For that matter, even if all of these segregated chambers are punctured the boat will still float since a considerable amount of residual air will remain trapped in the individual deflated tube sections.

The question of longevity always arises. Most people remember that Uncle Charlie bought an old war surplus inflatable thirty years ago, or perhaps picked up a cheapy in one of the discount stores a few years back, and the thing didn't last more than one or two seasons. This may well be true. Doubtless Uncle Charlie's boat was made of natural materials, like cotton or unprotected pure rubber, and these can deteriorate very rapidly when exposed to unsuitable conditions like too much sunlight or poor storage. Modern fabrics and coating are discussed in more detail in the next chapter, but suffice to say that new synthetics, developed during the past few decades, have changed the situation, so that fabric hulls often last as long as hard hulls, and even outlast them under certain conditions of use.

Little wonder that inflatables have been so wholeheartedly accepted by the Europeans, and that they have become a very significant and rapidly growing factor in marine sales in North America.

Super-stability and enormous carrying capacity are two unexpected benefits which inflatable owners quickly discover. (Novurania Inflatables)

Tough skinned modern inflatables are able to operate successfully even in extremes of cold or heat. (Bonair Boats)

Nevertheless, millions and millions of people still have doubts when confronted with a boat which is so radically different in design and concept. To a great extent inflatables are like olives. They are an acquired taste, and they must be sampled to be truly appreciated. My own experience is a case in point.

My initial involvement with modern inflatables took place in the late 1960's. At the time I was running scuba diving tours along the rugged western coastline of Mexico, in Baja California, and badly needed portable boats of some kind to carry customers out to the many interesting reefs and offshore islands. Baja is not a manicured country. In most places even a good dirt road is a surprise and a luxury, so trailered boats were out of the question, and car-toppers just couldn't carry the kind of payloads that scuba diving requires. It was essential that our boats be portable, stable and have large load carrying capacity.

My two partners were the ones who first suggested that we

use inflatables. Both of them were former members of the Navy's Underwater Demolition Teams (UDT), and had been trained to use inflatables for military combat operations. I was skeptical. I had never ridden in or even looked at, a modern, well-made inflatable, or one powered by a large engine. Somehow boats made of fabric did not sound substantial enough to withstand the kind of rough treatment that sustained commercial scuba operations would expose them to. Inflatables might be fine for the Navy where cost and longevity are secondary considerations, but for a business venture, where you expect the bottom line to show a profit, they did not sound practical. How long would they last under the constant exposure to strong sunlight, and what would happen to the seams and bottom after repeated launchings and recoveries through heavy surf and across rock strewn beaches? Could these small 14 and 15-foot boats really do what we expected of them? Would they be able to carry the heavy payloads we required, and be stable enough to counter

The military forces of almost all nations utilize inflatables for many of their water-borne operations. (U.S. Navy Special Warfare Group)

21

The author's first inflatable proved to be the ideal answer for his scuba diving tour business along the rugged coastline of Baja California in Mexico. (Don Hubbard)

the awkward movements of top-heavy divers preparing to get into the water?

Even in those days good inflatables were expensive, and with my doubts unresolved I was not prepared to commit a great deal of money on a gamble.

What solved the problem was a short advertisement in our local paper. Someone was selling a small, ten-and-a-half-foot, French-made inflatable sportboat with motor for just $400.00. This we could afford, so we decided to purchase this smaller boat to experiment with before passing judgment on inflatables and investing in a larger fleet. On our next trip south we carried this little fellow along, and put it through its paces.

The light weight and portability of the boat were as advertised. All of the parts for assembly and inflation fitted into two small bags. Our campsite on this initial experimental trip was at the top of a two hundred foot cliff, with a small, ill-defined goat trail leading down to the water. The deflated boat was easy to pack down this narrow path.

We located a level spot on the upper part of the beach, and were able to assemble and inflate the craft in less than fifteen minutes. The surf was moderate that day, and four people in our party picked up the boat, with the engine attached, and carried it out into the water to a point where it was floating easily. Here the boat was loaded. Into it went four 40-pound diving tanks, four 20-pound diver's weight belts, and finally, four big men, with an average weight of about 170 pounds. Total weight of the package, including engine, fuel, oars and anchor, was something on the order of 950 pounds.

Admittedly the boat was overloaded. Its rated operating capacity was around 700 pounds. Nevertheless, this buoyant little vessel floated easily, and had sufficient freeboard so that it did not ship water even as it pushed its way out through the low surf. There is no question that any hard boat with this kind of load aboard would have swamped very quickly, even without taking into consideration the difficult problem of balancing cargo and passengers to prevent tipping.

The tough fabric used in the construction of modern inflatables allows them to operate without damage even on rough unprepared beaches. (Don Hubbard)

From a diver's point of view the boat was a delight. Space was at a premium, it's true. A ten-and-a-half-foot boat should not be used by more than two people for scuba diving, but we were experimenting. By seating our divers two to a side, fully suited up, all that was required for exit was a simple backward roll. When backward rolls are executed from small hard boats, divers must roll off in matched pairs, one to a side, to prevent capsize. This was not necessary in our little inflatable. If one diver departed the boat, and his partner delayed, all that would happen is that the boat would settle slightly toward the overweighted side. There would be no danger of capsize. Furthermore, if someone was having equipment difficulties and needed to stand erect to make adjustments, this could be done with confidence, even when top heavy with tank and weight belt in place. The traditional instability found in small hard boats was eliminated.

We also discovered that the fabric hull was not made of the fragile stuff which I had anticipated. On the next four trips the boat was subjected to a lot of unplanned abuse. Expertise

Scuba operations involve a lot of heavy gear and top heavy loads. Inflatables are uniquely suited to meet these requirements and are the frequent choice of both professional and recreational divers. (Avon Inflatables Limited)

in surf work is a learned technique, and because of our errors the boat was constantly bounced off rocks and boulders on the beach. Any hard hull would have been badly damaged or destroyed, yet our resilient inflatable pontoons remained unscathed.

Testing for durability under the strong Mexican sun was a problem we could not solve. Only time could provide that answer, and we were in desperate need of boats. The hull of our boat was made of nylon fabric proofed with neoprene rubber, and had an outer coating of a substance called Hypalon. Hypalon was the material advertised as the protective agent, the one which would prevent damage from sunlight and exposure to destructive agents like gasoline and oil. What was it and would it do the job? Hypalon is a DuPont product, and a short query to that company provided me with the answers. DuPont sent me a pamphlet which described all of the properties of this material, rating it against several other similar substances from the standpoint of resistance to abrasion, ozone, oxidation and weatherability. Hypalon beat them all. The information I received convinced me that the materials used in the construction of our boat could easily cope with the tough conditions we were imposing.

Our small ten-and-a-half-foot inflatable proved to be a good investment. As a test vehicle it convinced my partners and I to embark on an ambitious boating program for our scuba tours, and ultimately led me to open a successful store specializing in craft of this type. It cured me of the "Rubber Raft Syndrome", and replaced it with honestly earned respect for inflatable craft in all their diverse sizes and shapes.

Not surprisingly, because of their versatility, the boats are used extensively for other than recreational purposes. Many are in operation throughout the world performing rescue services, and the military forces of all nations employ them in many different forms. Commercial river rafting operators use their special versions to carry enormous numbers of sightseeing passengers down some of the most precipitous rivers in North America. Many offshore oil drilling rigs keep them aboard for survival use, and from a less wholesome aspect,

Six French adventurers, using three inflatable boats, traveled 5600 miles from the Arctic Ocean to the Gulf of Mexico, via the lakes and rivers of the North American continent (June 12 - September 7, 1978). (Hutchinson Boats)

Stable, buoyant inflatables have proved to be the ideal answer for conservation minded Greenpeace volunteers who man them in open ocean to shield whales from the harpoon guns of whaling vessels. (Greenpeace)

the boats are valued by smugglers who appreciate their carrying capacity, low profile, poor radar reflectivity, and easy concealment.

Water-borne scientists and explorers have also embraced inflatables for their superior qualities. For sheer variety, few can match Captain Jacques Cousteau as he has cruised the world, studying the environment and filming his exploits. If you have seen his television shows you will most certainly recall his so-called, "speedy Zodiacs", in action. His men have been filmed chipping ice off these fabric boats in the Antarctic; riding alongside massive sperm whales; speeding down remote rivers searching for exotic forms of marine life; and threading through the sharp corals that surround distant atolls. It was Cousteau's wide television coverage that gave many Americans their first view of these small and different boats. Yet his activities are only a part of the spectrum of adventures in which inflatables have played a significant role. These include the crossing of the Atlantic Ocean from the Canary Islands to Barbados (1952); a Pacific crossing from San Francisco to Hawaii (1974); a descent down the backside of the Andes Mountains on the precipitous Urubamba River, from Cuzco, Peru at 12,000 feet to the upper reaches of the Amazon (1965); a trip via canal, river and open sea, from Brussels, Belgium, to Antalya, Turkey, a distance of some 3,400 miles (1971); a 5,600 mile cruise by three boats, via lakes and rivers from the Arctic Ocean near Alaska to the Gulf of Mexico (1978); and an almost endless succession of shorter, though no less spectacular feats by hardy men and women throughout the world. For sheer courage, add to these the operations of the Greenpeace organization, which uses high-speed inflatables, manned by untrained volunteers, to shield the rapidly disappearing great whales from the harpoon guns of Japanese and Russian whaling ships. All of this made possible by the truly amazing boats that have evolved over the last thirty years, blending good design, careful workmanship, and the use of modern synthetic materials.

Chapter 2

Looking at the Modern Inflatable

When you compare the modern inflatable to earlier boats
made of cotton and natural rubber you find that you are
looking at an entirely different animal. By using new synthetic fibers, coatings and adhesives, designers have been able
to solve the problems of weak seams and rapid deterioration,
which were characteristic of boats made in earlier years. The
soft, floppy little doughnuts, which could carry no more than
the smallest engines, and had a life expectancy of little more
than a year, have given way to tough, well designed craft,
capable of duplicating anything that a hard boat can do, and
with a life expectancy to match. Today's inflatable manufacturers turn sheets of fabric into boats which operate with an
absolute minimum of twisting and flexing, and which are
capable of mounting extremely large and powerful engines.
Strong fabrics, bonded with strong cement, have permitted
the use of much higher inflation pressures, and this has
resulted in greatly improved overall performance.

Modern materials have also given manufacturers much
more latitude in designing boats to meet specific needs.
Where once the only inflatable was a little oval "bath tub",

the buyer is now able to select a boat which has been tailored to meet his requirements. High speed sportboats, dinghies, river boats, kayaks and canoes, self-inflating life rafts, and even hybrid craft, with inflatable tops and hard bottoms, are available on the market today, and almost all of these can be found in a wide range of sizes and prices.

Each of the different styles of boats have individual characteristics, and if you are unfamiliar with inflatables a short guided tour will be worthwhile.

The 66-foot Amphitrité, the largest inflatable boat ever constructed, was used by Captain Jacques Cousteau to transport his diving saucer SP 300. Power was supplied by eight 80 H.P. engines. (Zodiac of North America)

SPORTBOATS — These boats have been designed to operate with high performance engines. The main buoyancy tube is "U" shaped, and it has a permanently attached wooden transom near the stern. Almost all have inflatable or wooden keels, to provide better directional stability and improve performance, and they almost always incorporate a sectioned wooden inner deck, both for rigidity and comfort at high speeds.

In size, production sportboats range from 9 to 28 feet, but the majority are from 10 to 16 feet in length. Generally speaking, the engine carrying capability is determined by the

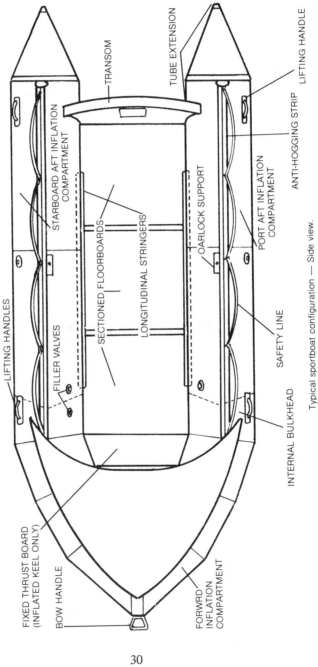

LIFTING HANDLES

FILLER VALVES

SECTIONED FLOORBOARDS

LONGITUDINAL STRINGERS

STARBOARD AFT INFLATION COMPARTMENT

TRANSOM

TUBE EXTENSION

LIFTING HANDLE

ANTI-HOGGING STRIP

PORT AFT INFLATION COMPARTMENT

OARLOCK SUPPORT

SAFETY LINE

INTERNAL BULKHEAD

FIXED THRUST BOARD (INFLATED KEEL ONLY)

BOW HANDLE

FORWRD INFLATION COMPARTMENT

Typical sportboat configuration — Side view.

30

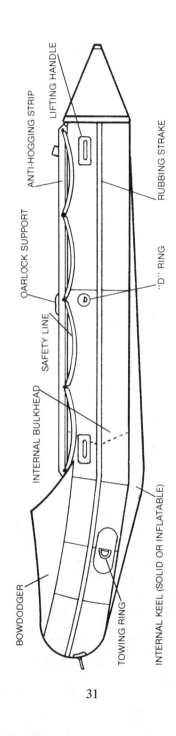

LIFTING HANDLE

ANTI-HOGGING STRIP

RUBBING STRAKE

OARLOCK SUPPORT

"D" RING

SAFETY LINE

INTERNAL BULKHEAD

BOWDODGER

TOWING RING

INTERNAL KEEL (SOLID OR INFLATABLE)

Typical sportboat configuration — Side view.

31

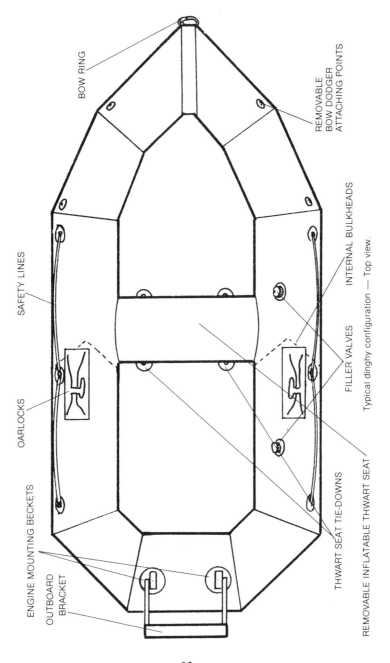

BOW RING

REMOVABLE BOW DODGER ATTACHING POINTS

INTERNAL BULKHEADS

SAFETY LINES

FILLER VALVES

Typical dinghy configuration — Top view.

OARLOCKS

ENGINE MOUNTING BECKETS

OUTBOARD BRACKET

THWART SEAT TIE-DOWNS

REMOVABLE INFLATABLE THWART SEAT

32

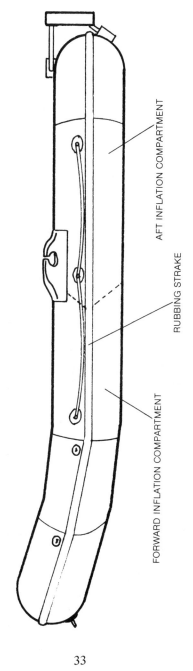

AFT INFLATION COMPARTMENT

RUBBING STRAKE

FORWARD INFLATION COMPARTMENT

Typical dinghy configuration — Side view.

33

overall size of the boat. The large Mark V Zodiac, which is 19 feet long, is able to mount a 115 H.P. engine, while even the smallest sportboats can be expected to operate with at least a 7½.

The advantage of the sportboat is in its performance, which is enhanced by the larger engine and by better hydrodynamic design, which permits these boats to plane easily. Their disadvantage lies in reduced internal space because of the transom position, and in the extra weight and bulk of the floorboards.

The sportboat is an excellent general purpose craft which will give a good account of itself in any boating role.

The giant 28-foot long Callegari Oceanic dwarfs the automobile it is carrying as cargo. This boat is capable of operating with up to 250 H.P. engines. (Callegari Inflatables)

DINGHIES — While the smaller sportboats can, and do, serve as dinghies, they are not the general choice of the yacht owner concerned with weight and storage problems. Most yachting people select the more compact and lighter all-inflatable dinghy. As a rule these boats are "O" shaped, and have a detachable bracket to mount the engine. Floorboards can be used, but are often avoided, since they are not necessary for the efficient operation of the boat.

The primary advantages of the dinghy design are light weight, stowability, ease of assembly on crowded decks, and more usable room. The disadvantages are limited engine size, and the sloppy feel of the fabric floor (although there are some dinghies on the market which incorporate an inflated floor that stiffens the deck, and adds both buoyancy and insulation.) Dinghies range in size from about 7 to 12 feet, and have normal payloads of 500 to 1200 pounds.

Riverboats have to be made tough to withstand the tremendous twisting and impacting forces created by rocks and turbulence in whitewater. (Maravia Corporation)

The Metzeler Spezi is a genuine whitewater kayak and its performance closely parallels that of its hard shelled counterparts. It incorporates a hanging fiberglass seat which also has a rim for attaching a spray skirt. The internal pressure is greater than on most inflatables in order to maintain longitudinal rigidity.
(Helmut Peters, Inflatable Boat Center, Santa Monica, CA)

RIVERBOATS — With the exception of the giant "J" rigs used in commercial river-running expeditions, most riverboats look pretty much like overgrown dinghies. Because these boats are almost certain to crash into rocks, run over shallows, and flex wildly as they run down the turbulent rapids, they have been designed for use without floorboards and without built-in transoms. As a rule fabric weight is heavier, and for boats which are going to be propelled by oars (as opposed to paddles) a rowing frame is added. The frame is normally custom made, and lashed to the top of the tubes.

Riverboats range in size from about 12 to 18 feet.

The Semperit Dolphin II was designed for whitewater use, but performs quite nicely for pleasant paddling sessions on flat water. (Lauren Hubbard)

CANOES AND KAYAKS — A number of companies produce boats which fall into this category. Some, like the Metzelers and Semperits, are very sophisticated in design and perform like their hard counterparts. Others have never overcome the problem of longitudinal stiffening, and tend to flex too much for efficient operation. Be this as it may, all of these boats provide a lot of good sport when used in rivers, surf, and other locations where there is action.

The primary disadvantage of all these craft lies in their light weight, which makes them somewhat susceptible to windage, and which reduces their forward momentum when paddled. Most of them are not a good choice for long range flat water paddling.

SAILBOATS — If your interest is in sailing, there are several makes of inflatable boats which provide this capability. Several companies (Metzeler, Sevylor, Semperit,

Many makes and models of inflatables offer sailing equipment as standard or optional equipment. Despite its blunt bow and light weight this Metzeler Maya performs quite creditably under sail. (Lauren Hubbard)

Hybrid boats combine rigid fiberglass lower hull with an inflated upper section. This permits the boats to ride more smoothly through choppy water while at the same time preserving the stability and buoyancy of the standard inflatable. (Don Hubbard)

Avon) manufacture sailing kits to use with their boats. Often these can be modified to use with other craft similar in size and shape. In addition there are some makes of boats which have been developed to be used primarily as sailing craft. The majority of the boats in the latter category are of the catamaran design, and they are usually the best sailers.

An inflatable boat with a sail will never perform like a Hobie Cat, but for the person who buys a boat because of its stowability, the addition of sailing equipment can add an entirely new dimension to his enjoyment.

HYBRID AND SPECIAL PURPOSE CRAFT — Under heavy sea conditions the bounce inherent in the normal sportboat can become so jarring that speed must be reduced. To offset this disadvantage hybrid boats have been developed which join a fiberglass bottom to a normal inflated sportboat top. This combination gives the hybrid the same smooth riding qualities of a hard boat, while retaining the stability, safety and buoyancy of the inflated craft. This combination works quite successfully, and because of this, boats of this type are often selected for offshore rescue work.

The obvious disadvantages are that the fiberglass adds weight, and the boats cannot be folded down into the compact packages that their all-fabric hulled brothers can. To some people this negates their value as inflatables because they must usually be carried on a trailer. Yet for those who look to inflatables for their buoyancy and stability, the smoother ride and higher attainable speed in rough seas make the hybrid a very desirable choice.

The Bonair Sea Sled is another unusual inflatable craft. The Sea Sled is made for the thrill seeker. This fourteen foot, missile shaped object is designed to be towed behind another boat at high speed, while up to four bucking and bouncing riders attempt to remain upright and on board. It provides some very wild thrills, and can keep a large group of people well entertained for the entire day.

The Bonair Sea Sled provides intrepid riders with some wild thrills when towed behind a high speed boat. (Bonair Boats)

Self-inflating liferafts pack down into small fiberglass containers or fabric valises, yet provide the seagoing yachtsman with a safe haven for himself and crew if he should lose his vessel. One couple, the Baileys, survived for 117 days in one after their sailboat was rammed by a whale and sank off the Galapagos Islands. (Avon Inflatables Limited)

SELF-INFLATING LIFE RAFTS — While not boats in the strictest sense of the word, life rafts have their place in the book of this sort. As a survival aid the covered self-inflating raft has no equal. When packed in their fiberglass or fabric containers, even the largest rafts occupy little space, but with a tug on the inflation lanyard these boats pop out and are ready for occupancy in less than a minute.

Fabric weight on life rafts is normally lighter than on regular boats. There are two reasons for this. The raft must be packed in a very small space, and when inflated and in use the raft is not expected to receive the same kind of long term abuse which a standard boat can expect.

Any good self-inflating raft is going to be expensive, but for the cruising sailor this item should be considered a necessity, and one of the normal costs of outfitting.

It is essential that life rafts be tested and repacked annually by an authorized service station. This inspection will verify that the raft is holding air properly, that the inflation system is fully charged and functioning, and that all supplies, which are packed inside, are still in-date and undamaged.

HULL FABRICS — Perhaps the most important consideration when purchasing an inflatable is the quality of the fabric. Poor fabrics invariably mean decreased performance, and often reduced hull life. Detecting poor fabrics is not always easy. Manufacturers of boats made of less durable materials are understandably very non-specific on the subject. There are some guidelines, however, for the novice trying to avoid the more obviously defective equipment.

All sorts of materials are being used for hull fabrics, but they can be divided into two main classifications: those which are reinforced with some kind of cloth material, and those which are not.

UNREINFORCED FABRICS — Unreinforced fabrics are almost invariably made of a compound of polyvinyl chloride (PVC) plastic, and boats made of this material are generally

41

The Sevylor K-88 is a multi-chambered sportboat made of unreinforced poly vinyl chloride fabric. Despite its relatively low cost it performs quite well with engines up to 10 H.P. The boat can also be fitted with sailing equipment. (Sevylor Inflatables)

of fairly simple design to permit mass production. The biggest single disadvantage to these boats is that unreinforced PVC material tends to soften and stretch, especially when warm, and because of this the boats are always a bit soft and floppy when used. However, material costs are low, and machine fabrication permits the boats to be made and sold quite inexpensively. Within certain parameters these boats are not all bad, either. There are some very innovative companies in the unreinforced PVC market whose boats perform well and offer reasonable longevity relative to cost. Sevylor, a French company, with a very extensive line of unreinforced plastic boats, has even introduced a line of high speed sportboats, which perform quite satisfactorily despite the relative softness of the pontoons. Two of these boats, the K-88 models, recently completed a 1,450 mile trip, from Cincinnati to the Gulf of Mexico via the Ohio and Mississippi rivers, to establish a record for river travel by inflatable craft for the Guinness Book of World Records. On the other hand, there are some very bad products being sold as well, and some of these are not only bad, but dangerous. Here are a few clues to help you detect poor quality boats of this type before you buy them.

As a rule the quality of an unreinforced vinyl boat will depend on: 1) the design, 2) the thickness and quality of the fabric, and, 3) the strength of the seams.

The worst design flaw is failure to provide proper chambering. Too often, in poorly made boats, the hull consists of a single undivided oval tube which, if punctured, will lose air and deposit the passengers in the sea. The easiest way to discover if a boat is chambered or not is to count the number of filler holes, or valves, which it has. If the main buoyancy tube has two chambers, then it will have two points of inflation. When making this count don't count floor or deck chambers. Even though these float it is unlikely that they will keep you from taking a bath if a main unchambered tube goes. As a guide it is usual for vinyl boats to have at least two chambers in the main hull, and one or two in the floor.

As mentioned earlier, boats made of unreinforced PVC material will stretch considerably when internal pressure is applied. This tendency becomes more pronounced as material thickness is sacrificed to profit. More importantly, thin material also means weaker seams with a greater tendency to split, even under light pressure loads.

Often fabric quality and seam construction can be determined by careful inspection of the merchandise. Begin by feeling the fabric. Boats made of good fabric FEEL tough. Even when uninflated the fabric feels heavy and remains reasonably stiff. Notice whether the fabric looks or feels excessively oily. Cheap PVC fabrics often have an oily look and feel to them, probably because of incomplete polymerization.

Closely examine the seams. These are almost always made by heating and welding the two sheets of material together with a bonding machine. On poorly made boats the machine often overmelts the vinyl to the point where the remaining material in the seam is thinner than either of the original sheets. A correct weld will be almost as thick as the combined original material.

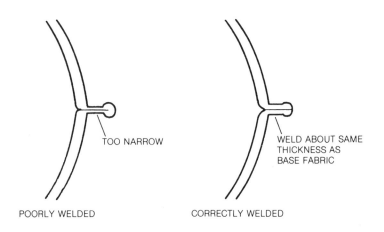

Heat sealed vinyl seams.

The final test is to look at the warranty. See if the manufacturer has enough faith and confidence in his own product to
warrant it against defects for at least one year. Find out when
the warranty begins. Sometimes it begins on the date the
merchandise leaves the factory, rather than on the date of
purchase. If the boat has been in the supply channel for any
length of time the warranty could have already expired.

A good quality boat made of unreinforced PVC material
will always be less expensive than a similar good quality boat
made of reinforced fabric. To my mind this is the primary
advantage of unbacked PVC. If you understand the overall
shortcomings of unreinforced materials: that the fabric will
stretch, and never become truly hard, and that even the best
electronically welded seaming is inherently weaker than the
lapped seams found on more sophisticated and expensive
inflatables, then perhaps one of these boats is for you.
However, if operating conditions include the probability of
heavy use, and if you require absolute reliability and long
term durability, then you will be better served by a more
expensive boat made of reinforced fabric.

44

This baby elephant seal probably wonders why his new-found mother is not delivering her usual supply of rich milk. Though not designed as a seal pacifier the tough inflatable skin was not damaged. (CDR R.L. Dale, USN (Ret.), Torgerson Island, Antarctic Peninsular)

The Navy's newest inflatable, made of Kevlar fabric coated with neoprene synthetic rubber. Kevlar, combining very light weight with great strength, is an excellent choice for inflatable boat construction. (United States Navy)

REINFORCED FABRICS — Reinforced fabrics for inflatable boats are made be impregnating or coating some form of cloth material with a suitable substance to prevent the passage of air. As we have said, unprotected natural fibers and coatings, like cotton and rubber, were not sufficiently durable to withstand weathering or the normal abuse expected in boating. This is not true with most modern synthetics like nylon, Polyester, Kevlar, neoprene, Hypalon and PVC. All are long lived synthetics now being used in the construction of inflatable boats.

Of the fabrics, nylon is the most frequent choice because of its lower cost, greater strength, and resistance to deterioration. Occasionally Polyester, i.e.: Dacron, or its European counterparts, is selected because of its very low stretch and higher melting point, which permits stronger hot vulcanization of the seams. Kevlar is also beginning to appear because of its very great strength to weight ratio.

The coatings which are applied to these fabrics are normally some form of synthetic rubber, like neoprene or Hypalon, or some mixture of polyvinyl chloride. Natural rubber is still occasionally used, but to be of any lasting value it must be coated on the exposed side with a tough synthetic coating, like Hypalon.

In inflatable boat literature the DuPont trademark "Hypalon" is the word most frequently seen. By definition, Hypalon is a chlorosulfonated polyethylene; a synthetic rubber made by reacting polyethylene with chlorine and sulphur. In fact, Hypalon, when properly compounded, is truly amazing stuff. Extensive tests and actual experience have proved that Hypalon is unusually resistant to damage from sunlight, ozone, flame, petroleum products, mildew, most acids, abrasion, flexing, color fading and low temperature. The result is an almost indestructible material almost ideally suited for use in inflatable boats. Trouble is, Hypalon, in its pure form, is not easily bonded with normal adhesives. For this reason, in most applications it is either mixed with neoprene synthetic rubber, or used as an outer protective coating over the more vulnerable neoprene. If properly compounded, the neoprene / Hypalon mixture seems

Running the rapid upstream is another alternative for inflatable owners. The lightweight resilient hulls bounce off obstacles, and the buoyancy and stability of the inflatable offer insurance if the engine should quit. This boat is made of nylon coated with PVC. Photograph was taken in Hell's Canyon on the Snake River in Idaho. (Bonair Boats)

the best solution, since it will approach pure Hypalon in durability, while the pure Hypalon outer coatings have a way of wearing or chafing off and exposing the more fragile material below.

Polyvinyl chloride (PVC) is the other primary coating material, and it is being used with considerable success by several inflatable boat manufacturers. In unreinforced sheet form PVC has some drawbacks as a boat building material, but as an impregnating or proofing material it is an excellent choice. It exhibits almost the same qualities as neoprene/Hypalon (It is somewhat more vulnerable to high heat and to some strong solvents), but it offers the manufacturer a much easier material to work with since it doesn't require as much preparation prior to bonding. Further, if the vinyl coated material is abraded, it can easily be recoated by the owner so long as the base material is intact. Recoating a chafed neoprene/Hypalon boat is a good deal more time consuming.

FABRIC COLOR — The best strengthening material for neoprene rubber is carbon black, consequently all of the earlier neoprene inflatables were either black or very dark gray. Dark boats suffer from two big disadvantages: they absorb heat from the sun which makes them uncomfortable to sit on; and they change pressure quite noticeably from day to night for the same reason. The introduction of Hypalon and vinyl has changed that, and now good quality boats are able to be reproduced in much lighter grays and a variety of colors. The light gray boats used to be the ones often seen, possibly because the popular Avon and Zodiac boats are this color and they have been around longer. Light gray has its advantages since it doesn't show dirt too readily, and it doesn't absorb so much heat that it becomes uncomfortable to sit on. Pure white boats are produced by some manufacturers, and these remain truly cool, but they tend to glare a bit in the sun, and they show dirt more. Colored boats offer the same advantages as light gray, and more and more of these are beginning to appear in this country as inflatable boating catches hold and new buyers wish to express their individuality. Additionally, many of the red, yellow and orange boats are purchased simply because they have greater visibility at sea.

COATING THE FABRIC — The technique used in coating, or proofing, the fabric is as important as the material used. If the impregnating substance is not properly bonded to the base it will tend to separate under pressure, especially at stress points like folds and seams.

Knife coating and calendering are the basic ways in which fabric is coated.

In knife coating the impregnating material is spread on to the base fiber with a device similar to a long, rigidly held, knife blade or spatula. The proofing material is thinned with a solvent so that it will flow easily, and then it is layered on, one thickness at a time, until eight to ten coats have been applied. Rubberized materials made in this way are almost always poorly bonded between layers because of the porosity

48

imparted to it by the thinning solvent, and later separation of the individual layers is common.

Vinyl material which is knife coated does not suffer from this defect because a different chemistry is involved. A PVC powder is mixed into a liquid plasticizer, which is then spread on to the base fabric. The coated material is then run through a long oven until the heat dissolves the PVC powder, and fuses it to the fibers in the fabric.

The calendering process is the very best way to coat rubberized fabrics. In this process the base material is run between two extremely heavy rollers (a calender), which compresses the proofing substance deeply into the cloth fibers, and essentially welds the materials together.

Equipment costs for buying and maintaining calendering equipment are high, and material fabricated in this way is always more expensive. For this reason it is rarely used to make low cost boats.

RECOATING DETERIORATED FABRIC — When boats made of natural rubber or a poor grade of neoprene begin to deteriorate, the skin develops an overall pattern of fine cracks, which permits air to seep through. Can a boat in this condition be recoated and brought back to usable condition? Well, maybe. If the problem is detected quickly, there are products on the market which can seal seepage holes in deteriorating fabric. Whether the effort will be worth the time and cost is doubtful. The problem is that cheaply made boats are exactly that, and if the fabric is deteriorating you can expect to find other related problems. As mentioned earlier, cheaply made boats almost always use inexpensive rubberized fabrics made by the knife coating process. This means that, in addition to the pattern of cracking, you will probably discover some degree of layer separation, usually at points where the fabric has been folded. Coating will not repair these areas. Additionally, you can expect that the fabric has also begun to deteriorate in the seams, where the recoat will not reach. The seam area will remain weak, and this may lead to early failure.

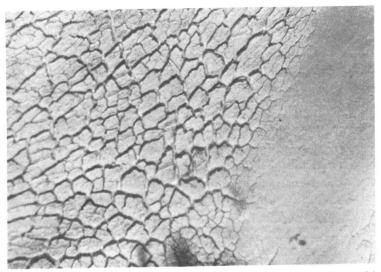

Deteriorating rubber develops an overall pattern of fine cracks which weaken the material and permit air to escape. Resealing the skin of a boat which has reached this stage is difficult and probably not worth the effort. (Don Hubbard)

Recoating is an iffy proposition, with no guarantees. If your boat is new, and the seepage is minor, then a new skin may prolong its life. On the other hand, you may recoat today, and have a split seam tomorrow. There is no way to know.

SEAM TYPES — There are three different ways in which seams can be constructed on inflatable craft. On quality boats, the preferred method is to lap the seam, one piece over the other, with a minimum overlap of one inch. With seams of this type the exposed outer edge should face aft to prevent lifting as the boat moves through the water. The edges of the seam may or may not be taped, but if they are not the inner edge is often sealed with a bead of silicon, or similar flexible material, to help retard wicking (see below).

The butt seam is very rarely seen since it is not as strong as the lapped seam and takes at least as long to make. Flanged seams are the least attractive of the three types, and must be

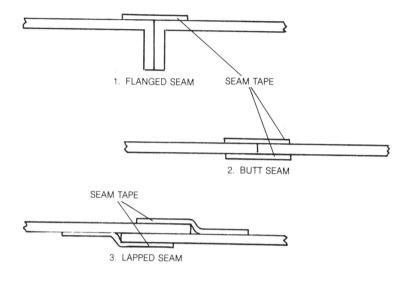

1. FLANGED SEAM   SEAM TAPE

2. BUTT SEAM

SEAM TAPE

3. LAPPED SEAM

Types of seams.

reinforced on the inside with tape to prevent separation under pressure. (Taping is not necessary on the flanged seams used on heat sealed unreinforced vinyl boats.)

WICKING — It is a fact that even on the best boats there will be some pressure loss if the hull sits inflated for any length of time. This is because air escapes, very gradually, by flowing along the strands of the base fabric, until it is finally released along some exposed cut edge. This process is called wicking, and it is normal. How much air loss can be expected? This will depend on a number of factors, including the size of the boat, the degree of initial pressure, the thickness of the individual textile strands, the amount of exposed cut edge (taped or sealed edges lose less air), and the degree and type of impregnation. Understandably, with that many variables there is no precise formula for calculating air loss. What is important, is that the boat should not soften to

51

the touch in less than five or six days. Beyond that there is no way of judging, since the rate of pressure loss often differs even in identical boats. Further, the pressure loss may be due to other factors such as improperly tightened valves, or contraction of the air caused by cooler temperatures. If you feel that your boat has an excessive drop in pressure, check these other possibilities before returning it to your dealer for a warranty claim.

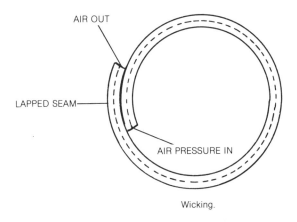

Wicking.

TUBE DESIGN — In inflatable sportboat parlance the terms "tapered tube" and "parallel tube" are often encountered. On the tapered tube boat the diameter of the tube in the forward end of the hull is several inches narrower than the diameter aft. In parallel tubes the diameter does not vary. Proponents of the tapered tube claim that by using a larger diameter aft they compensate for the weight of the engine, and the narrower tube forward provides maximum usable interior space. Those who favor the parallel tube claim greater longitudinal rigidity, and greater latitude in load placement. To some extent the arguments on both sides are valid, and may be a consideration to potential buyers with special needs. Generally, however, under normal operating conditions either type of hull will give satisfactory performance, and tube configuration should be of secondary importance in boat selection.

If a sportboat is properly designed, the tubes will extend beyond the transom for a certain distance. In a way this is wasted space, but it is essential to provide buoyancy for the engine, and to counteract the tendency of the bow to rear up when sudden power is applied. Compared to the horsepower of the engines which most of them can carry, inflatables weigh very little. Sudden application of power on a large engine creates tremendous thrust just below the stern of the boat and exerts upward leverage on the transom. If the tubes project sufficiently far aft, this leverage will be at least partially offset by their buoyancy, and unless there are extenuating circumstances like strong headwinds or extremely light loads, the boats should quickly stabilize and drop down into a plane. If the design is poor, and there is not sufficient tube buoyancy aft, the boat can very well perform a back flip and end up inverted.

The amount of leverage which a tube can counteract is one of the factors taken into account when an engine rating is assigned to the boat. As a rule, the greater the buoyancy behind the transom, the larger the permissable engine, and vice versa. This is one of the reasons why the maximum engine rating assigned by the manufacturer should not be exceeded.

The actual diameter of the tubes is another important consideration. Larger tubes mean greater payloads, better longitudinal rigidity, and higher freeboard. All of these are very desirable features. At the same time larger tubes add weight, are more expensive to build, and, unless beam is increased, they take up internal space. Thus tube diameter is a compromise, established by the characteristics which the designer is trying to build into the hull. This is a point for you, the potential buyer, to consider. The built-in characteristics of an inflatable hull may far exceed your needs. It may be tempting to buy a boat capable of mounting an engine of 65 H.P. with a carrying capacity of over 2000 pounds, but why pay for all of this if it will not be needed.

Tube stretch is another problem which inflatable builders encounter. Because of the tremendous leverage which the larger engines exert, the upper portion of the hull tubes is under considerable stretch stress. If this is not compensated for, the top of the tube will gradually lengthen relative to the bottom, and the bow will droop, causing the boat to hog. To offset this, many boats will have a four or five inch wide strip of material, called a hogging strip, cemented along the tops of the tubes. Usually this takes the form of an upside down "T", with the top of the "T" cemented to the boat, and the vertical portion punched with grommets for attaching safety lines. As a general rule, any boat powered by an engine of 30 H.P. or more should incorporate some form of anti-hogging feature.

CHAMBERING — Multiple chambers are to the inflatable what built-in flotation is to the hard boat. Chambering is essential to safety, and any inflatable boat which does not incorporate this feature should not be considered for purchase.

There are a number of ways in which chambering can be achieved, and these are illustrated below.

In the larger sportboats, and in many dinghies, chambering is most often achieved by the creation of internal bulkheads at intervals along the tube. These bulkheads are not flat walls. As a rule they are either cones or hemispheres. This design makes it far easier to achieve and maintain equal pressure in adjacent tube sections without repeated checks with a gauge. This is possible because the cone or dome will float fore and aft as pressure in one side or the other varies. With a flat bulkhead there would be no way to compensate for pressure differences, and the bulkhead would be under almost constant strain.

Since most people do not understand this fact about bulkhead design, they are often caused needless worry when they begin to deflate their boat. They release pressure in one chamber, and notice a pressure loss in the chamber alongside as the divider shifts to the deflated side. Depending on the distance that the bulkhead has shifted, the pressure loss in the inflated side can be quite noticeable. To the uninitiated this suggests that a leak has occurred in the bulkhead, and that the safety of the boat has been compromised, but this is not true.

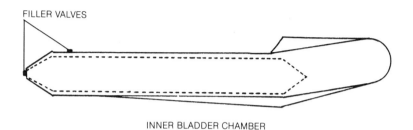

INNER BLADDER CHAMBER

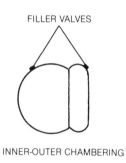

INNER-OUTER CHAMBERING

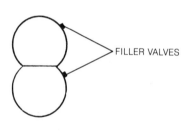

OVER-UNDER CHAMBERING

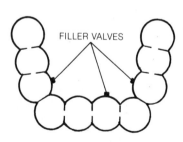

MULTIPLE TUBE CHAMBERING

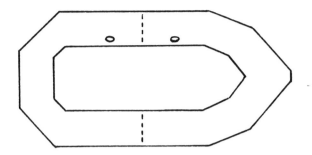

FORE AND AFT CHAMBERS

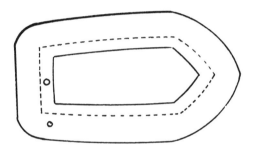

INNER AND OUTER CHAMBERS

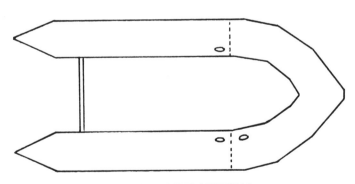

TRIPLE CHAMBERED SPORTBOAT

Types of chambering.

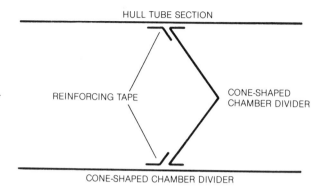

Chamber divider.

VALVES — Air is introduced and removed from inflatable boats by means of valves. How efficiently this is done is very much dependent on valve design. The valve must be sufficiently large to permit rapid air movement in and out, yet small enough to be unobtrusive when the boat is in use. Other requirements in a good valve include: high resistance to corrosion; low damage potential; simplicity and aesthetic appeal.

One of the most functional valve designs now in use consists of a threaded base, permanently attached to the hull, which accepts an insert (frequently made of plastic) to which the hose end connects. The bottom of the insert has a rubber diaphragm which opens and closes as the pump is operated. The diaphragm permits the operator to stop pumping, or even disconnect the pump hose, without loss of air pressure. A cap provides the final seal over the pump connection point once the hose is disconnected. The advantage of the valve insert is that it can be removed, leaving a much larger port for rapid deflation. Since it is possible to lose the valve insert, or to damage it, it is a wise precaution to carry a spare aboard.

There are many other valve designs being used on inflatable boats. Most work reasonably well but fail one or more of the major tests. This is no reason to reject these boats if they have other features which appeal to you. Most valve deficiencies are minor, and can be corrected by a simple maintenance program, or by accepting slower deflation and inflation times.

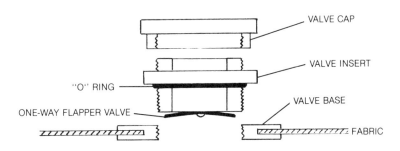

Typical valve with removable valve insert.

KEELS — Operating an inflatable sportboat without a keel would be very uncomfortable. Flat, sloppy bottoms are acceptable on dinghies which move slowly through the water, but at speed the flat bottom pounds badly, and directional stability is difficult to maintain. The keel serves the additional function of reducing drag by preventing the bottom from distorting inward as forward pressures build. Keels remedy these problems by forcing the loose bottom fabric downward into a "V" shape, which tightens it and gives it a better water entry.

Two basic types of keels have evolved, the hard keel and the tubular inflated keel. Both have advantages and disadvantages worth examining.

The hard keel is formed by placing a rigid longitudinal member, usually made of wood, between the floorboards and the fabric bottom. The keel is sectionalized into two or more pieces for ease in transportation and storage, but in use these pieces are solidly joined together to form a single unit. Boats which have hard keels almost always provide the passengers with a smoother ride, especially in short, choppy seas, because the hard keel has no inherent bounce to it. Boats with this type of keel have a more positive water entry and better turning characteristics since the fabric bottom is forced down into a sharper "V" shape, and hard keel boats also flex less because of the added longitudinal rigidity.

On the negative side, hard keels add a bit to the weight and storage space of the boat, lengthen assembly time, require more maintenance, are susceptible to breakage, and since they have little give, can contribute to tears in the bottom fabric. Furthermore, after a period of time the bottom fabric can stretch, and unless some adjusting mechanism is incorporated, the keel may begin to fit poorly, and performance will suffer.

The inflatable keel compensates for these problems, but has an inclination to bounce more, and since the "V" is less distinct, it slides more on turns and when running in high winds. It is also possible to distort an inflatable keel on really fast running boats when the external water pressure exceeds the internal air pressure. This distortion will permit the bottom to deflect inward and cause the boat to slow down as drag increases.

Which type of keel is best? Both of them are. It just depends on how you intend to use your boat. If storage space is critical, or if you will be doing most of your work on and off rocky beaches, then the inflated keel is probably the best answer. If you will be doing a lot of running in the open sea in choppy water, or if you are looking for the fastest top end speeds, then the hard keel will provide you with the best choice. The real truth is that both types of keels do many jobs equally well, and it is only in special applications where one or the other becomes more critically important.

The all-inflatable dinghy rarely has a keel as standard equipment, but these are sometimes added by owners whose boats have floorboards. Even though dinghies are inherently slow creatures, tightening up the bottom fabric can add a knot or two under power, and the keel does provide some additional directional stability. At least one manufacturer produces a dinghy floorboard with an inflated keel attached, but in most cases the keel must be fabricated by the individual boat owner. The easy solution is to force small diameter boat fenders between the floorboard and the bottom fabric. Any similar device will work so long as the material is soft and resilient. Dinghies are frequently used to transport passengers to unprepared beaches, and a solid keel may cause damage to the bottom if the boat is run up on to unseen rocks.

FLOORBOARDS — In sportboats the floorboards do not just provide a solid decking. They are an integral part of the overall design and essential to the proper functioning of the boat. The sectionalized boards are installed before air is added to the hull, so that when the tubes are inflated the boards are locked solidly in place. In boats with wooden keels the boards are usually attached to these. On all boats it is usual to incorporate longitudinal stringers along the sides. With all of these working together — inflated tubes, keel and stringers — the floorboards become locked together and are able to transmit the thrust of the engine from the transom through the remainder of the hull. Floorboards serve other functions as well. They counteract the tendency of the hull to hog, or otherwise flex, at high speeds; and the stiff boards also act as a backing for the keel, forcing it downward so that the bottom maintains a proper "V" shape. Lastly, the floorboards protect the passengers from injury should the fabric bottom strike some hard object.

When floorboards are used in dinghies, the primary function is to provide some substance to the otherwide floppy bottom. Without a solid decking the dinghy bottom resembles an underfilled water bed, and many passengers find this distasteful and bothersome, especially if water has gotten into the dinghy and pools around their ankles when they stand. Dinghy floorboards may also function to increase the speed of the dinghy when under power by stretching out the bottom and maintaining a flat, smooth surface.

A properly designed floorboard should be strong, light in weight, easy to remove and install, water resistant, and have a non-skid surface. In the larger sportboats this is not an easy combination to achieve. Because of their large size the boards in these boats often become extremely heavy and no longer easily portable. This may be important to you if light, folded portability is one of your requirements.

Varnish, or clear polyurethane, seem to be the favorite finishes for floorboards, and they shouldn't be. These materials are transparent, and when they are scratched the wood below absorbs water and becomes discolored. Refinishing boards in this condition is no easy task, and often not done at all, to the detriment of the expensive woodwork. It would be far more practical, and probably less expensive, to finish the floorboards with a few coats of high grade paint. Paint can be retouched in minutes and still look good. At least one company, Bonair, has taken this one step further, and coats their boards with a rough textured vinyl. This gives the boards a tough finish, which is durable, non-skid, and presents a very decent appearance.

TRANSOMS AND MOTOR MOUNTS — As previously mentioned most sportboats have permanently mounted transoms, and dinghies generally have some provision for mounting a detachable motor bracket.

On sportboats it is common to set the transom into an extruded rubber molding, which is then cemented to the buoyancy tube. This is strongly reinforced with glued fabric stripes on the sides and ends. Some manufacturers also add metal braces, which run from the upper edge of the transom to the floorboards. There is no objection to having these, provided they are mounted well to the side where they won't stub toes.

Outboard brackets are mounted on dinghies in a number of ways. Some are good and some are bad. The outboard exerts a lot of torque, and the attachment for the bracket takes a lot of abuse. The bracket mount must be strong, and well designed, so that the leverage of the engine will not twist it off the boat after a few starts. Use special caution with motor brackets which use screw-in oarlocks to hold one end in place. Occasionally, when the engine is started, the vibration, coupled with the upward leverage, unscrews the oarlocks and pops them out. This can easily result in a lost or dunked engine. With this type of mount the best insurance is to tie the oarlocks so that they can't rotate once the motor mount is in place.

AIR PUMPS — Air is the primary ingredient in an inflatable boat, and a good pump is an essential item. Despite their seeming simplicity, there is a lot of variation in both the efficiency and quality of pumps, and many of them are totally unsuited for use with inflatable boats. Bicycle and automobile pumps, for example, are very inefficient for boating purposes, since they are designed to deliver a lot of pressure but very little volume.

A larger diameter foot pump, or bellows, is the best choice for an inflatable owner. The bellows expands to a large size between strokes, which means that it will deliver a lot of volume each time it is compressed. Further, it is actuated by bodily weight, rather than by back and arm muscles. An important point when you consider that it may take 20 to 25 minutes of pumping to inflate one of the larger sportboats.

It is almost impossible to overinflate a good inflatable boat using a foot bellows. The pressure which any pump can deliver is a function of the piston size versus the force of compression. The piston size of a standard inflatable boat foot pump is large enough so that even the weight of a heavy person will be insufficient to cause pressure problems. This is not true in the case of some inflatable boat hand pumps which can easily achieve pressures of over ten pounds with very little effort.

Poor quality pumps and bellows, which cost little, often do little. Almost all good quality boats come with an efficient, well made pump as standard equipment. There are ways to check pumps, and it is a good idea to test before you buy. Be on the lookout for any of the following deficiencies: Recycling spring too weak for fast recovery after each stroke; fabric pump skirt not tightly secured to the bellows and leaking air; pump skirt of flimsy material which will disintegrate after a few uses; air intake valve not closing properly resulting in loss of air on compression; pump hose too short, too narrow, or so thin and flexible that it kinks. The pump gets the heaviest workout of any part on the boat, so this is no place to economize.

If you want to make life easy on yourself, buy a small electrically operated pump to do most of your inflating work. Generally these are small hand vacuum cleaners which have been adapted for the purpose. Don't buy a pump designed for inflating an automobile tire. These deliver pressure, not volume. Your electric pump will operate on 12 volts, and can be plugged into your cigarette lighter. Some are designed to operate on both 12 and 110 volts, so that they can be plugged into house current when it is handy. Don't expect your electric inflator to do the complete job for you. They deliver lots of volume, but rarely over one half pound pressure. Electric inflators will quickly bring your inflatable up to shape, and save you most of the work, but bringing the boat up to its normal operating pressure is still something which must be done manually.

What about inflating a boat at a gas station, or by using high pressure air from a scuba tank? These sources can be used, BUT ONLY WITH GREAT CAUTION, and only to the point where the boat is inflated, *but still soft*. Once a boat has been inflated to the point of hardness, the difference between three pounds and fifteen pounds pressure is hard to detect, and it becomes a simple matter to blow every seam in the boat. This has happened, and the lesson is expensive.

HULL FITTINGS — The hull is not complete until all of the fittings have been cemented into place. As a rule all inflatables will come equipped with a bow ring or handle, "D" rings or loops along the tops of the tubes with safety lines attached, and some type of oarlock mounting. Very often lifting handles are cemented to the outside of the hull, and additional "D" rings are positioned inside to aid in cargo tie-down, etc. It is quite important that all of these fittings be of good heavy construction if they are going to last for any length of time. Soft rubber handles, flimsy fabric loops, and then little wire "D" rings just don't make it.

CARRYING BAGS — One of the attractive features about inflatable boating is the ability to deflate and store your boat when it is not in use. To do this properly the boat must not only deflate and disassemble easily, but must reduce in size sufficiently to fit its storage bags. With properly designed bags this is not a great chore, but this is not always the case. Too often bags have been designed to fit boats when they leave the factory with all of the air vacuumed out. No thought has been given to the poor guy who will be pushing, prodding and kneading the thing, next to some boat ramp, trying to restuff it into a too small bag. Look the bag over when the boat comes out of its box. Correctly fitted bags will have some excess room in them when they come from the factory, and any straps or ties will have sufficient extra length to allow room for expansion.

Aside from fit, check the bags for fabric quality and strength. The material must be strong enough to withstand years of heavy use. Chafing is the name of the game as boats are loaded and unloaded and moved about in transit. Mildew will blossom on untreated canvas when someone forgets to thoroughly dry the hull before putting it in storage for three months. Any bag will have a short life under those conditions.

As with the boats, the best materials for carrying bags are the synthetics, like nylon, and they are better still if they have received a waterproof coating of some sort.

If you have a quality inflatable, the bags are important because they are protecting a large investment. Make certain that your bags are of good quality and have a proper fit, and use them when your boat is deflated.

Chapter 3

Selecting an Inflatable Boat and Motor

When you set out to select an inflatable boat, the most important decision you have to make is to determine what your intended primary use will be. Inflatables are versatile craft but no boat can do everything, and by defining your requirements you stand a much better chance of buying the correct one the first time around. This simple exercise will help you to eliminate a great many of the makes, models and styles of boats from consideration, a problem which often confuses first time buyers. By narrowing your possible choices to just a few boats you will be better able to compare the special features offered by each — cost, engine capability, ease of assembly, weight and size, accessories, etc. — to arrive at the boat you will eventually buy.

Defining your requirements does not necessarily mean that you must settle on one single role for the boat to the exclusion of all others. On the contrary, most people want a boat to perform in a variety of roles, and these are legitimate items to take into consideration. You may need a boat as a yacht tender that can also double as a diving platform; or you may wish to operate at high speed with a moderately powerful

Stores specializing in inflatable craft are common in Europe, and are now beginning to appear in many major U.S. population centers. By offering many different makes and models of these boats the retailer is better able to cater to the tastes and pocketbooks of a much wider segment of the population and offer better service. This store displays and sells Avon, Bonair, Boston Whaler, Campways, Metzeler, Maravia, Novurania, Sevylor and Zodiac. (Don Hubbard and Ocean Ventures, San Diego, CA)

engine, but still have a boat light enough to heft to the top of your automobile or motor home. Since individual needs vary greatly, the number of possible combinations is practically limitless, but they are all valid and should be considered when you go out shopping. Compromise may be called for, but inflatables have the ability to perform in many roles so it is likely that you will be able to find at least one which comes close to suiting all your needs.

Selecting a boat of the correct size is often a problem. Passenger and cargo requirements are apt to vary greatly from trip to trip, and you may be tempted to buy a boat that is designed to carry the maximum contemplated load. There are times when this is necessary, but the decision should be carefully justified against the additional costs in money, weight, assembly time, more powerful engine requirements, and storage space for the larger craft. Generally it is wiser to decide what your normal operating conditions will be and rely on the tremendous reserve buoyancy of the inflatable to accommodate an occasional extra payload. Often the larger inflatable boats tend to lose their charm after just a few sessions because of their extra weight and assembly problems. It is not unusual for the larger boats to end up on trailers because of this, and a trailer may be exactly what the owner was trying to avoid when he bought the inflatable.

What about cost? Inflatable boats vary in cost from very cheap to very expensive, and the performance of any given boat is usually directly related to its price. In inflatables you get what you pay for, almost without exception, and if money is no problem you can hardly go wrong if you buy the most expensive boat consistent with your needs. However, if you are like most of us there will be some disparity between what you want and what you think you can afford. At this point the cheap boats begin to look more and more attractive. The problem is, that in the long run the cheap boat may be far more expensive, in terms of dollars versus value and use, than the boat which is more costly. This is easier to understand when you consider all of the advantages you receive when you buy the better boat. Here are some of them:

Top quality material	Careful workmanship
Strict quality control	Innovative design
Higher inflation pressures	Much greater reliability
Good dealer network	Availability of parts and
Reliable warranty	accessories
Much higher resale value	Considerably longer life

When considering inflatables it is true that for two or three times the money, in any given size and style category, you will probably get eight to ten times the boat. A cheaply made boat which costs two or three hundred dollars and lasts for one or two years, is considerably more expensive in terms of use than one of the same size which costs six hundred dollars but still gives satisfactory service ten or twenty years from now. In the long run you will be wiser to defer your purchase until you have saved enough money to buy one of the better quality boats.

Avoid making a cost comparison between inflatables and hard boats of the same size. This comparison is not valid since an inflatable will usually have at least the same weight carrying and performance capability as a wood, metal, or fiberglass boat at least a third again larger. If you must make an inflatable/hard boat cost comparison, do it on the basis of capability. To find the size of an equivalent boat, divide the size of the inflatable by two and multiply the result by three. According to that formula you would compare a 12-foot inflatable to an 18-foot open hard boat or a 14-foot inflatable to a 21-foot hard boat. Admittedly this gets a bit tricky with larger boats, but the theory is generally valid. When based on capabilities the cost differential appears more realistic, especially when you then consider the related expenses of hard boat ownership, i.e. larger engines, trailer, remote steering, more fuel, etc. A good inflatable should not be any more expensive than any other boat which is able to carry the same payload, and when all the other hard boat expenses are added, the inflatable will almost always cost less.

It is important to note that cost is not the only criterion on which to base your choice of boat. There are some other considerations which will tell you very quickly whether you are looking at an inflatable of good quality. The most telling of these is the rated internal pressure which the boat is designed to operate at. Good quality boats made of reinforced fabric almost never operate at less than 2½ to 3 P.S.I. Some even go to 4 P.S.I. and higher, and in nearly all cases this pressure can be doubled without adversely affecting the hull. A well made boat can withstand these pressures because the impregnating material is properly bonded to the base fabric, and the seams have been put together with quality adhesives. Poorly made boats do not have these advantages, and you will usually find that they specify low operating pressures in the vicinity of ¾ to 1¼ P.S.I.

The operating instructions which the manufacturer supplies will also give you an indication of the overall quality of the boat. If there are heavy cautions to avoid spilling fuel, oil or grease on the fabric, you can only conclude that the impregnating substance overlaying the base material is of poor grade, and will deteriorate when exposed to these agents.

Finally, poor workmanship is symbolic of a poor quality boat. Boats made of reinforced fabrics are mostly hand made. Sloppy seams with excess cement splotched on by careless workers; woodwork that is bady finished; fittings that have been poorly positioned or sometimes not completely cemented down — these things reveal lack of care and supervision in the manufacturing process. Boats with these defects should be looked upon with suspicion.

The annual inflatable boat races in San Diego draw large numbers of participants and spectators of both sexes. Here a group runs for the ocean surf carrying a small riverboat which they must paddle to an offshore marker and return to the starting point. Versatility is one of the features which inflatables offer. (Lauren Hubbard)

USED BOATS — What about used boats? If the skin of the better inflatables is as good as its supposed to be, wouldn't a used boat still be a worthwhile buy? Of course it would! Used inflatables do come on the market, just like anything else, and if you can find what you want in good condition go ahead and buy it. If you are careful, and have done your homework, you should be able to save money, and still end up with a fine boat with many years of life left in it.

Understand that the above statement does not apply across the board. The cheapies we spoke about earlier are still a bad buy, and you must be cautious about paying too much for older boats made of unreinforced vinyl. In the latter case, *some* of these boats seem to harden and become brittle with age. Because of this they develop a susceptibility to seam failure which is often fatal to the boat, and whatever money you spend on the purchase will be lost. This is not to say that you must completely avoid buying used all-vinyl boats. Just examine the plastic carefully and keep your dollar outlay small to minimize your risk.

When examining a used inflatable boat there are two important points to check: Does the boat hold air, and what is the general condition of the skin, seams, woodwork and accessories. It is a simple matter to check both of these items at the same time. Assemble and inflate the boat to see that it will remain at, or nearly at, its original pressure for a least 24 hours, and as you put the parts together examine each one for wear or damage.

While you are making this inspection take a special close look at any patches which are evident. Mix a simple solution of soapy water and brush some over each patch (and any seams that might be suspect). If there are any leaks they will be easily located by the formation of bubbles. If you do find that air is escaping there is little point in continuing with your pressure check. Deflate the boat, patch the leaks (or have the owner do this), and then, after waiting for the cement to cure, reinflate the boat for the check.

If there is woodwork you can tell a lot about the boat's condition from this. Look to the floorboards. Are they cracked or badly worn, or are they beginning to delaminate?

Are the side stringers warped or split? Details like these will reveal to you how hard the boat has been used and what kind of care the former owner has given it. Check the transom. Is is still firmly anchored to the main hull tubes on both sides? Look under the transom, outside. Is it all chipped and worn away from repeated encounters with rocks and other hard objects? Carefully examine the thrust board. This is the board which is permanently mounted inside on most sport-boats with inflatable keels, and against which the detachable floorboards abut. See that the thrust board is firmly anchored in place on both sides, top and bottom, and that the fabric tabs which hold it in place are not ripped.

Internally, inspect the point at which the bottom fabric connects to the tubes. Inside where these join there is an overlaying strip of fabric which reinforces the joint. This is called the doubler, and it is cemented to the tube on the one hand and to the bottom on the other. See how much chafing has occurred to the doubler material due to excessive movement of the floorboard edges and the stringer. On boats that have seen hard service it is not uncommon for the doubler to be worn completely through and in need of replacement (expensive).

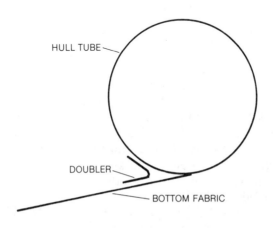

Doubler.

71

Look to all of the "D" rings and connecting fittings, like grommets, to see that they are securely attached and not ready to break off or missing. Inspect all of the accessory items which were supplied as original equipment. This includes the pumps, pump hose, possibly lines, oars, repair kit, and carrying bags. These should all be with the boat or the price should reflect their absence. If you think this is being petty, check the price of some of these items. A new set of jointed oars for some makes of inflatables can take care of the better part of a hundred dollar bill. Pumps cost between thirty and forty dollars or more. Carrying bags about the same.

What other accessories are offered with the boat? Electric inflator, launching wheels, box seats, floor coverings? The more of these you get for the price, the more you will save by buying on the used market.

What are the disadvantages of used boats? To begin with, you are completely without warranty protection. If you buy one through a dealer he might be persuaded to give you some form of protection, and you might even be able to work this into an agreement with a private owner. But most of the time you are left without recourse, and if the boat proves to be a terrible dud it is your loss.

Secondly, used inflatables do not come on the market all that often, so it may be a long wait and you may end up with the wrong boat, or one not consistent with your particular needs.

Finally, unless you exercise a good bit of caution, you may find yourself in possession of a stolen vessel. Because of their unique ability to deflate and store in small packages inflatables have become a good target for thieves. To the uninitiated most inflatables look pretty much alike. Fortunately, the Coast Guard and the various states require that inflatables be indelibly marked, somewhere, with a hull serial number. Usually this is on the transom, but sometimes it is stamped on the inflated tubes. Search for it. *IF THIS NUMBER IS NOT AVAILABLE DO NOT BUY THE BOAT.* Or at least not until you have been able to verify through your State's licensing division that the boat you are

Most modern inflatables are assembled by hand. Careful, neat workmanship is one good sign of quality. (Bonair Boats)

buying is not a hot item. As a used boat there should be a State registration number (provided the boat has been used with a motor or sail). This number is keyed to the permanent serial number on the hull. Many States record both registration number and serial number on a computer for easy recall. If you have one number you should be able to get the other, and if the boat if stolen the State will probably know that as well.

Buying a used boat is like buying anything used. You should approach it with caution and make your own inspections and decisions. There are good buys on the market for the intelligent shopper. But for the unwary there are many pitfalls, and as we said about cheap boats, a bad used boat can be more expensive, in the long run, than a good new one.

SELECTING AN ENGINE

A decent engine, nowadays, is apt to cost as much as the basic boat, so it is rather important to select the correct one the first time around. Of course, there is some latitude here. If you already have an engine and it is slightly too large or too small for your inflatable this is not absolutely critical. It is only when you go past a certain point that overall performance changes drastically and you become disappointed with your new boat. This is what we want to avoid, and why this section has been added.

Engine selection with inflatable dinghies is reasonably simple since the latitude of choice is small. Dinghy engine brackets are mounted outboard, and the usual attachment fittings are not designed for excessive stress. For this, and other reasons, dinghies are not capable of safely carrying more than a very light engine. In most cases this means a maximum of 3 or 4 horsepower, and a gross weight of 35 pounds or less. The manufacturer will usually stipulate this in the literature which accompanies the boat, and you can select your engine accordingly. But what happens if you already have a 6 or 7 horsepower engine which you would like to use? Assuming that the bracket attachments are sufficiently sturdy to stand the added strain, probably nothing. At least not so far as speed is concerned. Dinghies are displacement hulls. That is, they push through the water rather than planing on top. Displacement hulls have a maximum top speed beyond which even massive amounts of power will have little effect. Generally, top hull speed will be attainable with the manufacturers maximum recommended engine, and additional horsepower will add no bonus. But even if this were not the case you would still not benefit significantly. Why? Because dinghies are not reinforced longitudinally, and as soon as you pour on the extra power the stern will bend under, and the boat will begin to hog badly. Hogging deforms the bottom contour, adding massive drag, which again brings you back to that maximum hull speed. If you still wish to use a larger engine, you do so at your own risk. Avoid the temptation to use more than sufficient power to do the job. Keep a close eye on the motor mounts to make certain they are standing up to the extra power and weight. If you twist them off you will probably lose your engine, in addition to invalidating your warranty.

Ideally, the best choice for a dinghy engine will be the largest engine that the manufacturer recommends. This will give you the power to push your maximum load, with a little extra to spare for those days when the wind is whipping up the anchorage. If you are tempted to buy a smaller engine, do so only if the savings in cost and weight are significant. Generally the price differential between 2, 3 and 4 H.P. engines is small, and the savings over the life of the engine will be too minor to make a difference. At the same time, the extra power may come in handy one day.

There a few precautions which you should take when using an outboard with a dinghy. *ALWAYS* secure the engine to the hull with a strong piece of line, or a chain, just in case the motor bracket should decide to part company with the boat. Secondly, when towing your dinghy, take the engine off. Dinghies are light, and high winds or high seas can flip them. Many an engine now rests on the bottom because this basic rule wasn't followed. Finally, it is a very smart move to remove the engine from the dinghy when you are going to be at anchor for any length of time. This will protect you from loss through theft, which is not uncommon, and will also preclude dunking the engine should the rear chamber of your boat lose pressure.

High speed inflatable boats are unique because of their weight, shallow draft and extreme buoyancy, so if you have arrived at any notions about correct engine size for inflatables derived from familiarity with hard hulls, forget them. When an inflatable sportboat is traveling on a plane at high speed, it has been estimated that the engine is at least half again as efficient as it would be on a hard boat. The way to check this is to compare the wakes of the two different types of boats when they are running with the throttle open. Invariably the hard boat will produce a much larger wake.

Since the wake consists of waves produced by the energy of the engine, a larger wake means more energy uselessly expended. An inflatable owner can use a much smaller power unit than his neighbor with a hard boat, and still expect the same performance. This means lower fuel bills, less overall weight, and less space for storage, all of which contributes to the portability of the inflatable boat.

What size engine should you choose? Sportboats come with a maximum rated horsepower just as dinghies do, but there is much greater latitude to choose from. It is not unusual to find 12½-foot sportboats which are rated to use engines of 35 to 40 horsepower. When you consider that 12½-foot boats weigh in the vicinity of 130-140 pounds, you can appreciate that a 35 to 40 horsepower engine is relatively large. In fact, if the boat is lightly loaded, the thrust of one of these engines can often push the boat beyond safe operating limits. Realistically, there are very few situtations where maximum horsepower is of any value.

As a rule a considerably smaller than maximum engine will be more than adequate, and will also offer considerable economy in basic cost, fuel consumption, and overall size and weight. It is usually wisest to buy the smallest engine which will be consistent with your needs. There are no precise guides, but the following table will give you some idea of the performance you can expect with various boat and engine combinations.

Their light weight and buoyancy makes inflatables very efficient and economical power boats. The lack of wake behind this sportboat indicates that very little energy is lost in the creation of waves. (Bonair Boats)

APPROXIMATE PERFORMANCE IN M.P.H.

BOAT SIZE & WEIGHT	NO. OF PASSENGERS	6 H.P.	10 H.P.	25 H.P.	40 H.P.	55 H.P.
9'0"	1	6	15			
69 Lbs.	2	5	7			
	3	4	5			
10'6"	1	14	19	25		
100 Lbs.	2	10	16	23		
	4	6	7	21		
12'6"	1		18	25	31	
144 Lbs.	3		15	22	26	
	6		7	18	23	
14'6"	1		16	23	29	38
219 Lbs.	3		14	20	26	34
	6		6	16	23	24
16'6"	2		14	20	22	30
262 Lbs.	4		12	17	20	26
	8		5	14	18	23

Table courtesy Avon Inflatables Limited

Here are a few additional considerations in engine selections:

Engines are heavy, and the more powerful they are the heavier they get. Generally, when an engine weighs more than 100 lbs. it becomes too heavy for the average person to easily heft working alone. If this is a consideration, then your maximum size engine will have to be in the 20-25 H.P. range. This amount of power is adequate with most inflatables in most applications. If you have to push heavy loads, but still want to use a 100 pound or lighter engine, then examine the possibility of using a more efficient propeller for the job. Most engine manufacturers supply lists of recommended propellers for specific jobs or load conditions. There are three variables in propellers: number of blades, overall diameter, and pitch. For heavier loads and slower speeds a three bladed, smaller diameter, lower pitched blade is called for. It is not unusual for outboard motor owners to have more than one prop with different characteristics so as to obtain maximum efficiency under varying load conditions.

Most engines are available in either long or short shaft versions to cope with variables in transom height. With inflatables it is extremely important that you follow the manufacturers recommendation concerning shaft length. As we mentioned in Chapter 2, the sportboat transom is set into an extruded rubber molding which is then cemented to the hull tubes. This mounting procedure is quite strong enough for the maximum rated engine with the prop running at a known distance below the boat. Using a longer than recommended shaft, however, introduces a new factor into the equation, and in all probability almost doubles the leverage stresses. If you continue with this arrangement for any length of time it is very likely that you will find your transom beginning to tear away from the hull.

Dinghies, incidentally, almost all take standard shaft engines, and even these often run too deep. Outboard brackets on dinghies are usually lower than the transoms on most small hard boats. As a rule this positions the engine too deeply in the water for efficient operation because the extra depth causes excessive back pressure on the underwater exhaust. Most manufacturers will indicate correct running depth for the engine in the owner's manual. Since the problem of low transoms on dinghies is not uncommon, there is usually some adjustment which can be made, or spacer which can be added, to bring the engine up to proper running depth.

Many conventional outboard engines can be converted to jet drive by purchasing kits made for this purpose. These jet units can be used on inflatables where conventional propellers would be dangerous, or where frequent operation in shoal waters would damage a normal prop. While there are some differences in performance (there is about a thirty percent power loss when converting to jet), the greatest conversion problem for the inflatable owner lies in the modifications he must make to the transom. Jet units on standard shaft engines require an approximately 20-inch high transom for proper positioning. This means that height will have to be increased some five inches, and then heavily reinforced on both sides. Aside from the trouble and cost which this modification requires, the added material means extra weight, and substantially increases the difficulty in rolling up the deflated hull.

Satisfactory performance with a jet drive unit depends upon an uninterrupted stream of water reaching the jet intake. When inflatables are being operated with insufficient internal air pressure, jet units will give disappointing results. This is because bottom flex will permit air pockets to form, breaking the water flow. When a jet unit is used on an inflatable, a tightly inflated keel (or properly fitted wooden keel), and tight hull tubes, are an absolute necessity.

Because jet conversion units are expensive and difficult to mount they should only be considered where essential for safety or where propeller operation is not possible because of water depth.

Electric starting units are a necessity with very large engines, but they are rarely required with the small engines most used on inflatables. This is a happy circumstance, because it means less equipment to purchase, carry, connect and store on the boat. Nevertheless, some owners will require electric starting, either for convenience when their boat is equipped with a forward steering (and starting) unit, or because one of the operators is physically unable to pull the manual starting cord through. If this is the case, then it is important that the battery, which supplies the power, be strongly encased in a leak resistant battery box with a well fitted and vented top. This, in turn, should be strongly secured to the deck, preferably well aft where there is a minimum of bounce. It is extremely important to minimize the possibility of splash, spillage or leakage of the battery electrolyte, since this is a strong mixture of acid and water that can burn the skin, damage the clothes and dissolve metal. Sealed, spill-proof batteries are now available, and though more expensive, these are an excellent choice for use in inflatable boats.

Remote steering equipment is another bit of gear that can usually be eliminated on an inflatable boat. Ordinarily there is very little need for the use of remote steering with engines

79

of 50 H.P. or less. The torque on these smaller engines is not great, and it is a very simple matter to control them manually. Beyond 50 H.P. engine manufacturers rarely make provision for other than remote steering, and the installation then becomes a necessity. However, it is possible to install this equipment on most smaller engines if you feel that it suits your mode of operation or will offer some special advantage.

Depending on the remote steering unit you examine you will find some sort of pedestal or thwart is required which must be mounted or attached to the boat to support the steering wheel and engine operating controls. From these, control cables will run along the deck, or along the tops of the tubes, to the engine. Often the steering cable is attached to the transom by means of a small bracket from which it obtains the leverage necessary to move the engine. The engine control cable is connected internally inside the engine casing. There is no quick disconnect for either the steering or control cables, so if deflated portability is a consideration know that you will be faced with a certain amount of inconvenience each time

Remote steering equipment can be installed on most engines if needed. This type of steering is convenient for water skiing and similar high speed operations, but causes some loss of interior space and adds to assembly and disassembly time. (Bonair Boats)

you assemble and disassemble the boat. To this disadvantage you may add the loss of internal space in the boat, as well as weight and cost. Unless there is a compelling reason to install forward steering equipment right away, you would probably be wiser to try operating with manual controls first. You can always shift to remote steering later if the manual system proves to be inconvenient.

When you buy a new engine take the time to read the owner's manual carefully. Every engine has its own peculiarities, which the manufacturer tries to explain in the instructions. Usually the very first portion of the book will deal with proper break-in procedure. Heed this information carefully, since the life expectancy of your new and expensive piece of machinery depends on it. Normally there is not much that you will be required to do beyond adding some additional oil to the fuel, and perhaps using slightly reduced power settings for the first few hours of operation. This permits the newly machined parts to wear into place with proper lubrication, and without excessive and damaging heat. You will also probably be required to change the lower unit lubricant after a certain period of time to remove oil which might have become contaminated with small metal particles from the breaking-in. Whatever is required, following the correct break-in procedure more than pays for itself in the additional years of life which it can add to the engine.

In any engine, lubrication is of prime importance. The function of lubrication is to reduce the friction between moving parts of the engine. In two-cycle engines, such as outboards, lubrication is accomplished by adding oil to the fuel. The exact ratio of fuel to oil will be stated in the owner's manual and may vary from as much a 10:1 to as little as 50:1, depending on the design of the engine. The important point is that you should not run the engine with fuel which contains less than the amount of oil specified. To do so will result in overheating which can lead to burning, scoring, or even fusing, of the two adjacent parts. If you err on the side of too much oil this is far less of a problem. Aside from a bit of excess smoke, about all that will happen is that you will get some extra carbon build up on the piston and cylinder head, and your spark plugs may eventually become foul. Under the circumstances, if you are unsure about whether you have added oil to your fuel, go ahead and add more. The absence of oil in the fuel can destroy the engine, while excess oil can't.

An important bit about mixing. More than one engine has been damaged because the oil was poured into a dry empty tank before adding the fuel. When this is done the oil clings to the dry sides and bottom of the container, and only a certain percentage of this will release and go into solution when the fuel is added. The result is an oil-shy mixture with attendant problems. The correct procedure is to add some fuel to the tank, pour in the oil, mix well, and then add the remaining fuel as required.

The type of oil you use is also a consideration. Because the oil is introduced and burned with the gasoline, special two-cycle oils have been formulated. These have special additives to keep the engine clean and minimize the build-up of carbon and sludge on the pistons and spark plugs. Two-cycle oil is quite commonly available, and can be found anywhere that normal engine oil is found, as well as in shops specializing in two-cycle engines. As a temporary measure, if you can't find two-cycle oil then use any good grade of oil with a viscosity of S.A.E. 30 or better.

Before you put your new engine in the water there is one bit of preventive maintenance which is easy to accomplish and which will pay very large dividends in engine reliability and life. Remove the casing which surrounds the powerhead and thoroughly spray the exposed area with silicone lubricant, or if this is not available, with one of the oil based sprays like WD-40 or LPS. This coating will protect the engine from corrosion and acts to insulate all of the exposed wires, terminals, etc. Respray the area periodically as needed, usually every six months.

There are several precautions which should be observed when mounting the engine on the transom of a sportboat. Perhaps the worst thing that can happen is for the engine to detach itself from the boat and sink to the bottom. There are several things which you can do to prevent this from happening. Securely tightening the clamping screws with two hands is one obvious answer. But in most cases the engine should also be bolted on. Bolts take a few minutes to install, but they can save an engine which might otherwise go over the side.

Avoid using the detachable vinyl or rubber pads which are sold to be placed under the engine to protect the transom from becoming scarred. These have a tendency to slip in rough water, or on fast turns, and can result in a lost engine.

The motor tilt should be adjusted so that the engine is vertical when the boat is planing. As a rule this can be accomplished by adjusting your tilt setting so that the engine is in the full down position. The angle of the engine will not look right in this position when the boat is at rest, because the boat will be floating in the water in a nose high attitude, but when the boat is planing the nose drops and the transom lifts. This movement should provide enough angular change to position the engine correctly.

Cavitation is a common phenomenon which you may experience. You will be running through the water at planing speed, when all of a sudden the engine will rapidly increase its R.P.M. and thrust will drop off. What has happened is that in some way air has gotten around the prop, and without solid water to provide resistance the propeller blades will begin to spin wildly. Cavitation happens to nearly everyone occasionally, but is should be no more than that. Assuming the prop to be balanced and blemish free, cavitation is most often caused by seaweed or other debris being caught in the lower unit of your engine. This disturbs the water flow and introduces air. Removing the foreign matter will usually solve the problem (normally the easiest way to do this is to put the engine in reverse). However, if this does not cure the situation, there are three other possible causes. Your tilt angle may be incorrect, your boat may be running under-inflated, and/or your engine may be riding too high on the transom. Correcting the tilt angle is a simple matter, as we described in the preceding paragraph. Low pressure, especially low pressure in an inflated keel, can cause cavitation by permitting the bottom of the boat to become soft and floppy. In this condition it will undulate and permit air bubbles to become trapped in the water flowing aft to the propeller. Adding air to the underinflated chamber is the correct, easy, and usually effective solution.

If you have exhausted all of the foregoing solutions to your cavitation problem without success, it is probable that the engine is riding too high on the transom. This permits the anti-cavitation plate (the flange which projects outward on either side of the shaft, just above the propeller) to skip along the water surface where it picks up air. Ideally, this plate should run about a quarter inch under water. You can check this by watching the plate as the boat races along at high speed. If the plate is not running down in the water, then you must take whatever action is necessary to lower the engine until it is. The difference between good and bad can be very slight — as little as an eighth of an inch. If you are satisfied that your engine is seated firmly down as far as it will go, then you must modify the transom to lower it the additional amount necessary. On wooden transoms the easiest way to accomplish this is with a belt sander. The belt sander works quickly, and does a neat and easy job which can be refinished quickly with a can of spray paint or varnish.

ONE FINAL CAUTION — Since most owners deflate and store their inflatables when not in use, it follows that their engines are frequently removed from the boat and carried from place to place. Accidentally inverting the engine during this process, so that the powerhead is below the prop, has been the cause of some rather expensive damage which could easily have been avoided. Modern engines are designed to discharge exhaust gases underwater to cut down on noise. *If the engine is water cooled,* the exhaust is introduced into the water jacket, where it is then carried below the surface. When the engine is stopped and removed from the boat, there is always some excess water trapped in the cooling jacket. It is also quite probable that one of the exhaust ports will have remained in the open position. *THIS IS A DANGEROUS COMBINATION,* because if the engine is inadvertently turned upside down, the residual cooling water will flow backwards into the open exhaust port and flood the cylinder.

If the engine is stored in this condition damage can be very extensive, and an overhaul costly. It is perfectly acceptable to lay an engine in the horizontal position if you wish to store it on its side. Just be careful to keep the propeller unit even with or below the power head when the engine is off the boat.

Chapter 4

Care and Repair

Once you have selected the correct boat to meet your needs, your next move is to make certain that it gives you the maximum amount of pleasure with the minimum amount of fuss and bother. The purpose of this chapter and Chapter 6 (Technique), is to provide you with all of the information you will need to enjoy long years of safe and simple boating pleasure.

Always begin by reading the instruction book that comes with the boat. Every inflatable is different, and the manufacturer will try to clearly outline in the owner's manual all of the special procedures which apply to his particular model. This information will usually be brief, but techniques of assembly, disassembly, repairs, cleaning, and any special precautions, should be covered. Reading the manual will give you a good starting point on which to build further knowledge.

Before you unroll your new boat and begin pumping air into it, take the time to look it over in the stowed position. See how the factory has folded everything and stowed it in its bags. This is an important step that is rarely mentioned in the

Inflatables are easy to use and maintain, but there are shortcuts which will reduce your maintenance efforts and let you spend more time enjoying your boat on the water.
(Hutchinson Boats)

owner's manual. Later, when the time comes to repack the boat in its bags you will be thankful for the time spent doing this. Disassembling and stowing the boat may sound very simple in the instruction book, but it rarely is, especially on the first go-round. Note how the pontoons have been folded, how the hull has been rolled up, what kind of knots have been used, the order that the floorboards have been stowed in, and where the accessories are positioned. This initial look should answer all of these questions, and the answers may not be found anywhere else.

Another very good idea is to pre-inflate the hull, without the woodwork, and let it remain in this condition for twelve to twenty four hours before you assemble it for the first time. New boats need to be stretched a bit to allow all of the rigid parts to assemble easily. The boat may still go together without doing this, but pre-stretching the hull simplifies matters.

While you have the hull inflated on this initial pre-stretch, lubricate the inside, where the fabric floor is attached to the tubes. This will permit the newly varnished woodwork pieces to slip into place much more readily when you begin to put the boat together. There are a variety of lubricants you can use, but one of the least expensive and readily available is nothing but plain old cornstarch. Its only drawback is that the powder is a bit messy. Talc is more expensive, and also messy. If you prefer a lubricant which won't show try silicone spray or ArmorAll (more about these later). *DON'T* use petroleum based lubricants! These are sometimes harmful to the fabric, and will often stain.

ASSEMBLY — The actual assembly of the boat is rarely much of a problem provided you take your time and carefully follow the manufacturers directions. In all probability this first assembly will take at least twice as long as it will once you have learned the procedure. Don't become discouraged by this, it happens to all of us.

The floorboards must be inserted into the hull while it is partially or completely deflated. While you are doing this you may have to step into the boat once or twice. Hull fabric is certainly not fragile, but it will be damaged if your weight is concentrated on any sort of sharp projection. For this reason select a flat area in which to work, and be certain that it is free from sharp rocks and other items which might cause damage.

The floorboards in most boats have to be forced into place against the stretch of the hull. This is normally done by using your bodily weight or some sort of levering device. A good tight fit is necessary so that the boards transmit thrust evenly through the boat. Don't think that you have been given the wrong size floorboards if they don't pop in on the first try. After you have used the boat a few times everything will begin to fit better.

Installation of the longitudinal stringers is often one of the most difficult parts of the assembly process, especially if they are the type which fit along the sides of the floorboards (as opposed to those which attach on the top of the boards). You can often greatly simplify stringer installation by placing an oar lengthwise under the boat, about ten or twelve inches inboard from the floorboard edge. This will raise the boards slightly and level them. This procedure usually lets you roll the stringers into place with little further fuss.

Once you have your floorboards in place, and any other woodwork positioned, you can begin to inflate the boat. If you are using a powered low pressure air source, like one of the commercial electric inflators, open the valves as widely as possible to reduce back-pressure. Often this will mean placing the valve in the deflate position where the maximum aperture is achieved. With the valve in the wide open position you will fill the hull much more rapidly and put the pump to much less work.

You can usually tell when a low pressure electric pump has reached its pressure limit by the distinct change in sound which it emits. Check this by holding the running pump against your hand for a minute. As the pressure backs up the pump will begin to give forth a higher-pitched whine. When this happens while filling the boat it is time to switch to the manual pump. The function of the electric pump is to move a mass of air rapidly and effortlessly, but it cannot deliver enough pressure to tighten up the hull to operating pressure. Always change pumps as quickly as possible to avoid losing air.

Your owner's handbook will specify what the boat's proper operating pressure should be. Depending on the make, if it is a quality boat, the pressure will run anywhere between 2½ and 4 P.S.I. (this does not apply to the unreinforced plastic boats whose hulls tend to stretch and whose seams are weaker). If the boat has been supplied with a pressure gauge, check your progress as you go along. Remember, many gauges will not even begin to register until the hull is quite firm to the touch. More than one good gauge has been erroneously returned to the supplier for this reason.

What do you do if you have not been supplied with a pressure gauge? There are always a few clues to tell you when you have reached correct inflation pressure. To begin with, all of the wrinkles in the skin of the hull should disappear. Wrinkles form in the fabric when the hull has been folded down for storage. These are not damaging, but they are persistent, and usually remain in evidence until the boat is quite well inflated. Secondly, the hull should not feel at all soft to the touch. Push down on the inflated hull with all your weight with your fingertips spread. The fabric should barely give and no more than the slightest depressions should form.

The boat should not bend or flex excessively when you are using it. This is another certain clue to underinflation. After a few tries on the water you should have a good idea how hard your boat should be.

Finally, as we mentioned when we discussed pumps, it is almost impossible to overinflate a good boat when using a foot pump simply because of the physics of the thing. Lay into it until the back pressure on the pump is very obviously causing it to compress slowly. At that point you will be very close to the correct operating pressure.

There are a few special factors to consider when inflating your boat. Air heats when it is compressed which causes it to expand, and it also heats and expands when it is exposed to the rays of the sun. On the other hand, contact with cold water will chill the air in the hull making it contract. For these reasons you should introduce just a bit more air pressure to the hull than is required — perhaps a quarter to half pound. This will not hurt the hull, but it will compensate for this normal contraction when the boat is launched and keep the boat at its normal operating pressure.

Conversely, if you are inflating your boat at home and plan to carry it inflated to some mountain lake at higher elevations, keep the pressure at a low level to allow for the expansion as you drive up into the thinner atmosphere.

Heat expansion is also a problem with black boats, especially if you pump them up during the cooler part of the day (or when it is overcast) and then the sun comes out. With the sun shining on it a black hull will absorb heat very rapidly, and in great quantity, especially when the boat is on a light reflecting surface like a beach. The resulting pressure increase is often sufficient to overstress the material or seams, which can burst. Fortunately, this is rarely a danger with good boats made of gray or other light colored fabric, since with these the heat absorption is less.

PUMPING THE BOAT TO THE CORRECT HULL PRESSURE IS ONE OF THE MOST IMPORTANT STEPS IN THE INFLATABLE BOAT ASSEMBLY PROCESS. An underinflated hull greatly reduces performance, and often results in damage to wooden parts which are designed to rely on correct hull pressure for a part of their longitudinal rigidity.

TRANSPORTING — While most inflatable owners transport their boats deflated and stowed in their carrying bags, it is not at all uncommon to see them moved from place to place completely assembled, either on car top or on a trailer. Both methods are quite acceptable and effective, provided that you follow a few common-sense rules.

Cartopping is a favorite method, particularly with boats in the 12-foot and smaller sizes. Boats larger than this can sometimes be carried on top of a vehicle, but the increased weight of the hull and wooden parts makes getting them up there more difficult (there are easy top-loaders on the market which can assist here).

Certainly the greatest danger when cartopping is that the boat will come loose while underway. For this reason it is absolutely essential that good strong lashings be used and that these are correctly fastened. *No less* than three lines should be used: one from the bow of the boat to the forward part of the vehicle, and one each across the bow and the stern. Racks are not usually necessary since inflatables ride well if placed directly on the car top. It doesn't matter very much whether the boat is upright or inverted, although it is usually more convenient to get the boat up and correctly positioned on the car top in the upright position. But beware of rain unless you have good open drains. The additional water weight will not only make the boat difficult to get down, but can also cause the roof to buckle.

Wind resistance is the biggest problem with car-topped inflatables. The boats are light, but they present quite a bit of additional surface to the airstream. This is especially true in gusty crosswinds which can badly buffet a vehicle with so much additional sail area. Use caution on wet or windy days. When conditions are not favorable it is usually much smarter to deflate the boat and transport it in its carrying bags.

Car-topped boats, and also those on trailers, are very vulnerable to chafing, either from the tie-downs or from friction with the vehicle. Correctly positioned padding will prevent a lot of this from happening, and the use of webbing in place of line for tie-downs will help.

As a general rule you should avoid car-topping the boat for excessively long distances. The continued buffeting by the airstream over a long period of time will eventually cause your tie-downs to loosen. When this happens the boat will begin to move about and chafing is almost inevitable.

Their very light weight makes car-topping of smaller inflatables a favorite means of transportation. (Avon Inflatables Limited)

Many inflatables, particularly the larger models, are towed along behind the car on a trailer. Actually, unless you especially bought your inflatable for its stowability, trailering makes a lot of sense. Carrying the boat on a trailer provides that much more space in your car for additional people or extra equipment. And the boat itself can be used to carry some of your light but bulky items. Make sure that these are well secured and have no sharp edges to cause chafing. Most importantly, trailering saves you the trouble of assembling and disassembling the boat every time you use it and leaves you more time to enjoy the water.

It should be far less expensive to buy a trailer for an inflatable than for a hard boat. Unless you plan to pull something especially large like a Mark V Zodiac or the very large Callegari, with a powerful engine, or one of the hybrid boats with a fiberglass bottom, you can get away with a very simple trailer rig. Keel rollers, winches, tilting beds, brakes, forward dolly wheels, load equalizing hitches; these can all be eliminated for all but the very largest boats. With most inflatables the smallest and least complicated trailer in any given line will be perfectly adequate.

The type of boat supports, or mounts, which you install on your trailer can be very simple. For boats which lack keels, or which have keels which can be deflated, the easiest thing to do is to make a flat bed of plywood or masonite and rest the boat directly on that. If your boat has a hard keel then padded bars or stringers are the best solution. Whatever system you use be certain to provide adequate support for the transom, particularly if you plan to trailer your boat with the motor mounted in place.

If you plan to trailer your boat on long trips, or if you plan to store your boat and the trailer outside, then a good overall cover is a worthwhile investment. The cover will prevent the accumulation of dirt, water, leaves, and other debris on the inside of the hull and will make using the boat that much more pleasant. It will also help prevent premature weathering and deterioration of your expensive woodwork.

With or without a cover it is always a wise idea to open your transom drains, if you have them, so that any moisture which might enter the boat will find a quick exit.

Whole books have been written on the subject of trailering boats, but all that is intended here is to briefly discuss trailering as it applies to inflatables. However, it is appropriate to mention that the addition of a trailer to your car raises a whole series of new considerations. Not the least of these are lower speed limits in many states, possible special insurance requirements, changed vehicle handling characteristics, and additional safety problems. You should consider all of these items before you buy a trailer, and if you still decide to go this route it will pay you to do a bit of extra studying on trailer technique for the sake of safety.

Launching wheels are accessories which are available for several makes of boats, and which can be made to work on almost any wooden transomed sportboat with the installation of special wheel brackets. The larger wheels, such as those made by the Bodge and Zodiac Companies, will raise the transom sufficiently high so that a standard shaft length engine can be lowered to the full down position without touching the ground. With wheels of this size the whole unit appears to be a trailerable assembly. For very short distances on smooth and level ground this is true. The purpose of the wheels, after all, is to move the boat from its point of assembly into the water. What the wheels are not intended to do is trail the boat at high speed down the streets of your town to the water. To begin with this is illegal since the boat is not registered as a trailer. But it is also rather bad practice because the mounting brackets are not designed for this type of strenuous use. It is quite possible that sooner or later one of the brackets will detach from the transom, and it is a certainty that heavy fabric damage will occur to the inflated hull as it is dragged along the pavement. Additionally, the wheel bearings are not made for high-speed operation and can be destroyed by the excess heat build-up that occurs. Short trips at slow speeds are all that the launching wheels are designed to provide.

DISASSEMBLY — Disassembly is, in general, little more than a reversal of the assembly process, nevertheless, there are some procedures that can make your job easier and save you trouble later on.

If you are able, it is always easier to clean your boat before you deflate it. This way you can stand it up on its transom and flush all of the sand and debris out, aided by a hose and gravity. Abrasive materials, like sand, gravel and shells, are especially damaging to hull fabrics, and extra care should be taken to see that these are removed. Also, pick up or flush away any bits of seaweed, paper, fish scales, mashed sandwiches, or other items that will hold water or decompose in the rolled up hull. If you are unable to clean the boat at the disassembly site, reinflate it at home, without its woodwork, and clean it out there.

Needless to say the whole disassembly process will be a lot easier and cleaner if you can locate a good flat grassy area in which to work.

The first step in the actual disassembly process is to release the pressure by opening the valves. On a properly inflated boat it is always a surprise to see the force with which the air initially rushes out of the hull. The noise, alone, is certain to cause every head in the vicinity to turn. If your valve is one of those with a removable insert which is taken out to release the pressure, keep a firm grip on it as it is unscrewed. If you don't, when the last thread disengages any loosely held detachable valve insert will be blown out of your hand and become a flying projectile. The force is often sufficient to propel the insert twenty to thirty feet. Since valve inserts are expensive, and sometimes hard to find, it is sensible to hold on to them tightly as you unscrew them from their base.

Deflating the boat can also put the chamber separators under considerable strain when pressure is suddenly released in one chamber and not the other. The seams of the separators have been reinforced to withstand this under normal circumstances, but it can become a problem when the day has been extremely hot and the internal pressure in the hull

95

has increased well above normal. In this situation it is a good idea to reduce pressure gradually, so that the separator shift is not too violent.

Once your valves are open, and your hull begins to deflate you can begin removing the internal woodwork. Normally, your first step will be to remove the longitudinal stringers which connect the individual boards. On boats where these are mounted on top of the boards this is usually a simple procedure. Once the pressure is released top mounted stringers generally lift right out. This is not so with many of the stringers which are formed to fit along the edge of the boards. Very often these have been jammed into place by the pressure of the surrounding hull, or if the boat has been in the water for any length of time, by the swelling of the wood. To counter this problem lift the stringer off the deck by placing an oar under the boat. Take the other oar and while standing on the opposite side of the boat rap the reluctant stringer sharply several times with the oar end. This should dislodge the sticking piece and permit you to finish the job by hand.

Once the stringers are removed, and any other connectors unfastened, the floorboards should pop out or lift out rather easily. Clean them if they need it and then stack them in their carrying bag while the remaining air bleeds out of the boat.

If left alone most of the air will evacuate from the hull simply because of the weight of the fabric. However, there will always be some residual air which remains trapped inside the hull. The easiest way to work this out is to roll the boat up, little by little, and sit on it. If you have an electric inflation pump with a deflate position this will speed the process considerably. Don't vacuum the boat completely flat right away or you will have difficulty positioning the fabric for final folding. When the two sides of the collapsed tube are in direct contact, and vacuumed tightly together, the fabric can't slide against itself. This makes it almost impossible to fold correctly for rolling. Instead, use your electric pump to remove about three fourths of the air, position your tubes, and then finish the deflating.

Once the boat is deflated you must roll it up tightly enough so that it will fit into its carrying bag. If your boat has a permanently attached transom, this will establish the minimum size package attainable. Fold the projecting ends of the tubes around the back of the transom, then flip the remaining loose hull tube material inward, towards the center, until the bottom fabric is visible. At this point your collapsed boat will be laid out lengthwise, but should be no wider than the widest part of the transom. Now, using the transom as a card, roll up the boat and tie it.

With dinghies it is common to make a three-way fold by positioning one tube inboard on to the fabric floor, and then laying the other tube on top. This three-layer sandwich is then folded into thirds again, and tied prior to stowing in the bag.

When you plan to stow your boat for any appreciable length of time you should be certain that the hull is both clean and dry. Be especially careful to remove any oil, grease or tar, which will almost surely stain the boat and which might cause longer term problems.

It doesn't much matter how you position the hull for storage, whether stacked flat or on end, so long as it will be protected from damage. The usual precautions are necessary: watch out for nails, sharp rocks, projecting wall fittings, etc. which might cause tears in the fabric. Keep it out of the line of traffic so that it will not be stepped on or climbed over by everyone in the family. Use special precautions with pets, and don't stow it where there are rodents. Both categories of animal have been known to chew on inflatable hulls, often with disastrous results to both animal and hull. Avoid hot water pipes and heating ducts which might cause burns, and electric motors which generate large amounts of rubber damaging ozone. Nowadays theft is another problem. Inflatables are conspicuously theft prone. Lock up your boat is a secure place.

Keep all of your equipment together: hull, floorboards, accessories, engine, fuel tank (but if this is full of gasoline empty it into your car or use it to kill the stray grass along the

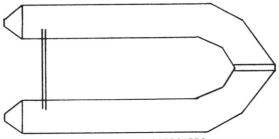

1. DEFLATE — REMOVE FLOORBOARDS

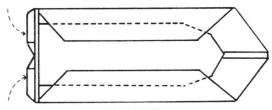

2. FLIP LOOSE FABRIC INWARD —
   BEND TUBE EXTENSIONS AROUND TRANSOM

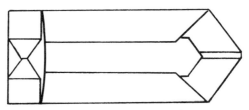

3. USE TRANSOM AS CARD TO ROLL BOAT

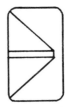

4. FINAL PACKAGE — USE BOW LINE TO TIE

Folding a typical sportboat.

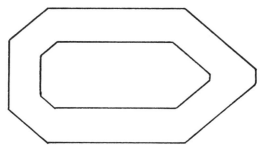

1. DEFLATE — REMOVE BOARDS IF USED

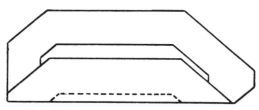

2. FOLD ONE THIRD OF BOAT INWARD

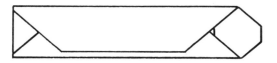

3. FOLD SECOND THIRD OF BOAT ON TOP OF FIRST

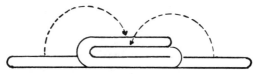

4. FOLD ENDS IN TO FORM PACKAGE —
   TIE WITH BOW LINE

Folding a dinghy.

borders of your garden). With everything in one location you will be reasonably sure to end up with your complete unit when you next reach the the water's edge. It is a very good idea to make a list of all your equipment to use both as a check list and in case of loss.

What about stowing the boat inflated? This works fine, but reduce the internal pressure somewhat to permit the elasticity of the fabric to relax and return. Many owners hang the inflated boat on straps from the overhead. This keeps it out of the way and provides protection from the animals.

If the boat is going to be out of service for any length of time you should check it over to see if there is any necessary servicing, repair or replacement which should be accomplished.

Your point of main concern will practically always be the woodwork, if there is any. Wood always seems to get scarred up with use and will require periodic overhaul. If you stay on top of this the effort will be minor, especially when compared to the problems which most hard boat owners face. But if you wait until your wooden parts are almost destroyed before beginning to rehabilitate them you may wait too long. Be particularly on guard against moisture which can cause dry rot and delamination of your expensive floorboards. Each piece of wood should be thoroughly dried and then recoated with a suitable finish.

Your valves should be inspected and lubricated if they are beginning to stick, or if any corrosion is evident. Look to all exposed rubber parts (almost all boats have some, such as rubbing strips, cone tips at the ends of the pontoons, certain types of oarlocks, valve and bailer diaphragms, etc.), and go over them with a good rot preventative like Armor All. See to all the lines, "D" rings and handles, and replace or repair any which are beginning to fray or tear loose from the hull. Finally, lay out all of your accessories and see if any of these require work. Your inflation pump is particularly vulnerable and important, and will lose efficiency very rapidly if the valves leak or if tears develop in the skirt.

If you take care of your routine maintenance as it is required, and before problems develop, the annual cost to you should be no more than a few hours of your time.

HULL REPAIRS — Good inflatables are no more prone to damage than hard boats, but accidents do happen and repairs do sometimes become necessary. There are many ways in which injuries can be inflicted on inflatable hulls. There are possibilities of punctures, cuts, tears, burns and abrasion. Weakened or overpressured fabric can burst, seams can split, or wooden parts can begin tearing loose from the hull. It really doesn't matter what has happened, most damage can be repaired provided you have the proper materials and an understanding of the correct technique. Despite all of the different damage possibilities, repair almost always reduces down to the problem of cementing fabric to fabric or fabric to wood.

Every inflatable boat should come with a repair kit, and the materials which these contain are usually adequate to repair most small damaged areas. For larger problems you will have to supplement your kit by obtaining additional fabric and cement. These can be gotten from your dealer or by writing to the manufacturer or importer. The biggest difficulty which confronts most beginning repairmen is the brevity of the repair kit instruction sheet. Improper technique is almost always the cause of the failures in repair work. Fortunately, correct repair procedures are easy to learn provided you have good instructions and you take the time to follow them.

Even though different fabrics sometimes use different cements or require different types of preparation prior to repair, there are a few common rules which apply universally. The most basic of these is cleanliness. Cement will not adhere to surfaces which are covered with dirt or grease or oil. Even the small amount of oil on your fingertips can be enough to botch the job. Clean the area surrounding the damage with a good detergent and water, and then swab it with a good cleaning solvent like acetone (*CAUTION:* some solvents will damage hull fabrics — test first). Keep your fingers off. If the book says to test the cement before uniting the two parts, tap it with your fingernail rather than the soft fleshy oily underside.

Moisture can also cause problems with adhesives. Dry the area to be patched thoroughly. Use a hair dryer, if you have one. And don't forget to dry the inside of the hull if the hole is large enough to admit water. Try to avoid outside repairs on rainy days, or any time when the humidity is high. If this is not possible then figure out some way to keep the airborne moisture level low. At home the hair dryer will help. If you are out on a trip then rig some sort of canopy to keep falling moisture off, and do your repairs near a good sized fire with enough reflected heat to keep the parts warm and dry.

Finally, the importance of surface preparation cannot be overemphasized. No matter what type or make boat you are working on, some type of preparation must be accomplished prior to the application of the cement. The fabric may just need a good cleaning, but more often the material will require thorough sanding or abrading as a prerequisite to effective repair. Whatever is required, lay into it and do it well, or your work will have little chance of success.

If prepared patches have not been supplied and you have to cut your own, be generous. No simple puncture should have less than a two-inch diameter patch, and three inches would not be out of line. Patches which cover larger rips and gashes must have at least two inches of lap on either side and at either end of the damaged area — and even more for very large cuts.

For both practical and aesthetic reasons patches should be cut with some symmetry and have rounded corners. The corners of sharp angular patches are too exposed, and tend to scuff up easily. Also, unevenly cut patches look bad, and reduce the future resale value of your boat.

The cement you use should be fresh and flow freely. Cement does go bad in tubes and cans, even if they haven't been opened. Some companies date their containers because of this, but that is not always the case. Under normal circumstances you can expect your cement to last at least two years, provided that it has not been opened. However, never go on a long or important trip without checking the condition of your repair materials. If you discover that your repair cement has congealed when you are stranded on the upper reaches of Lake Manitoba, you will be faced with a bit of a problem.

As mentioned, most repair kits are adequate for routine work. Still, it doesn't hurt to augment them to help simplify your job and to guarantee better results. To my knowledge acetone is never supplied with repair kits, but it works so well as a cleaner that it probably should be. Acetone should be used sparingly, as it will attack some plastics, and as mentioned earlier *all* new solvents should be tested on some inconspicuous and non-vital area before using. However, Bonair, whose boats are made of PVC impregnated fabric, claims that a light solvent attack by acetone is permissible as a means of surface preparation on their boats; and the author has used it on several different makes of unreinforced plastic PVC hulls with good results.

Toluene and Contact Cement Thinner, which contains toluene, are two other products which are interchangeable, and which are handy when working on Hypalon or neoprene boats. Either can be used as a cleaning agent for surface preparation (sparingly), and they both work quite well to remove excess adhesive (most kinds) after the patch is in place.

For larger repairs, where sanding is required, an electric drill, with a fine to medium grit padded sanding disk, can be extremely helpful and will greatly speed the job of preparation. Practice with it first so that you develop a soft and controllable touch. If your machine has a variable speed control, set it to a fairly low RPM. Back your fabric with a hard and smooth surface to prevent high and low spots which cause uneven sanding. Always work slowly when using power tools, and when in doubt stop and finish the job by hand.

Most punctures are easy to repair. The exceptions are those which lie on a seam, or which are tucked away in some inaccessible location. We will talk about these later. For the normal puncture the procedure consists of laying a patch over the area to be repaired and tracing around it with a grease pencil or a soft, dark lead pencil (ball point pens work, but it is difficult to remove the ink at clean-up time). While you have the patch in place mark a few reference lines from the patch on to the hull. These will help later in alignment. If you have several patches number both the patch and the area to be patched so that they will be correctly mated when final contact is made.

Do whatever preparation is required for the type of fabric you are dealing with, but stop about a thirty second of an inch *inside* the tracing line. This will compensate for fabric stretch once the repair is completed and the boat is reinflated to normal operating pressure. Don't forget to prepare the underside of your patch at the same time.

With PVC materials all the preparation that is usually required is a thorough cleaning with solvent, while on neoprene/Hypalon hulls a thorough buffing with sandpaper is necessary. If your hull is one of those with pure Hypalon overlaying neoprene then you will have to remove this upper layer to insure an effective bond. Check your owner's manual to see what they recommend. If they say to remove the Hypalon layer, then *remove it,* don't just scratch away at the surface and hope. The cement will not adhere unless the job is done properly.

Apply your adhesive in a thin and even coat to both surfaces, and allow this to dry until it is no longer tacky to the touch of your fingernail. If your directions call for it, apply a second coat (although this is rarely necessary if the first coat has been laid on properly). Again, let this dry. Now, using your reference lines, apply the patch, very carefully and gently. Once the patch is in place, check the alignment. If it is not correct, carefully remove it and begin again. When you are satisfied that the patch position is correct, apply pressure to firmly bond the two cemented surfaces. Begin at the center of the patch and work outward using any smooth hard tool. The butt end of a screwdriver works, and so does a kitchen spoon held in your hand with your thumb pressing down in the bowl. Be certain to work all the bubbles out as you rub down the surface. Finally, to achieve a good workmanlike job, clean the area around the patch, before the adhesive hardens, with whatever solvent is called for.

Let the patch cure for a least two hours, and then test by inflating the boat to a bit lower than normal pressure. Swab the patch with soapy water, and see if any bubbles form. If you must use the boat at this point, do so with the pressure reduced. The cement will continue to cure for several days until it achieves maximum bonding strength. Application of full internal hull pressure too early will usually result in leakage.

When you are working on a puncture in the hull the above procedures are necessarily carried out with the boat deflated. If you are adding accessory items like "D" rings or handles it is often easier to work with the boat fully inflated to its correct operating pressure. Doing this will give you a smooth and solid surface to work on and will help to insure correct positioning of the work. If you do work on the hull while it is inflated you should continue your surface preparation clear out to the traced patch outline since no further fabric stretch should be encountered.

With larger repairs the actual cementing technique will remain the same. The only real variation will be in the size of the patch, plus a few additional steps to insure a strong air-tight bond.

Any repair which is over an inch long should be patched both inside and out. The inside patch not only adds strength, but the internal air pressure forces it against the hole, or cut, making a more effective seal.

Inside patches take a bit of doing because so much of the work must be done by feel and often through a small hole. All of the usual patching rules apply. The inner surface must be clean and dry and prepared in the normal manner. Apply the cement to the patch (but not to the hull yet), and gently roll it so that the cemented sides do not touch. The rolled patch is then gently pushed through the hole and unrolled, cement side up, inside the boat. Now, working through the hole, move the patch about until it is located in the proper positioning for cementing. With this accomplished, apply cement to the inside of the hull, and by some means hold the two apart until the required drying has taken place. Finally, and carefully, lower the hull fabric onto the patch, and if still in position, apply pressure. Finish the repair job by applying the outer patch in the normal manner.

With very long rips it is sometimes a good idea to stitch the seam before applying the outer patch. If you plan to do this, do not apply pressure along the edges of the rip when you install the inner patch. In this way the edges of the rip can be lifted so that your needle can engage the material. Use small stitches, but pick up enough fabric so that your stitches do not pull out when internal pressure is applied. The principal objection to stitching is that the stitches raise the area slightly, and interrupt the smooth and even contact of the outer patch with the hull. This makes the repair more obvious, and makes it more difficult to achieve a continuous air-tight seal. You must compensate for this by making your outer patch overlap a bit more, which you should do in any event with a large tear. Three inches of overlap to a side is not too much on large repairs, and four is preferable.

Repairing leaks which are right next to, or which intersect lapped seams is one of the biggest problems which you are likely to encounter. This is because it is almost impossible to apply an airtight patch which must pass over that slightly raised edge. Invariably the air will find some way to run along the seam, in one direction or the other, and escape. Nearly always the only real solution is to raise the seam, using heat, apply the patch, and then recement the seam to the new patch. Unfortunately this advice only applies to the neoprene/Hypalon boats, since the lapped seams on PVC boats cannot be lifted by heat or any solvents. On boats of this type you must use other techniques. Obviously, since the problem is to make a patch jump a ridge then the problem can be minimized if the ridge is reduced in height. This can be accomplished using sandpaper or a pumice stone, but this is the hard way, since a fairly large amount of material must be disposed of and hand labor does not make for even work. Usually the best bet is to reduce the area with a carefully wielded disk sander, or with an electric Moto-tool, using one of the broad emery wheel points. You will have to position the fabric so that it forms a convex curve. This will make the ridge accessible, and minimize the risk of contacting the surrounding areas. Cover the area above and below the part to be worked on with masking tape, or some thin protective coating. It doesn't have to be too heavy, and it shouldn't be, or it will interfere with the work.

Once you have your material positioned, slowly and with great caution, begin to bevel the area to be patched. Work from the top downward, trying to produce a gentle slope extending from about one half to three quarters of an inch above the ridge down to its edge. Don't bevel above the ridge beyond the area where the fabric is lapped and is of double thickness. Above all, take your time, and check your progress after each stroke. The area you are trying to reduce is thick since it consists of two layers of cloth. It can easily stand to lose a bit of skin. But the fabric above and below the lapped seam is only single weight, and a heavy run over it with a powered abrasive wheel may easily compound your patching problems.

Ideally, your grinding will eliminate the ridge entirely, but this is not likely. Usually some slight rise will remain, but hopefully this will be insignificant, and with pressure you can force the patch down and obtain good adhesive contact. Part of the trick is to apply the adhesive a *bit* heavier than usual along the ridge area. This will help form a more level base, permitting better overall surface contact for the patch. If you do use additional adhesive let the patch cure for a few days before testing the boat under pressure. The thicker cement will contain more solvent and hence the curing time (the time for the solvent to evaporate) will be longer.

On occasion wooden parts of the hull must be recemented to their fabric bases. The actual cementing technique here does not vary from that used to join two fabric pieces. Apply cement, one or two coats as called for, let dry and unite the pieces. What usually complicates this process is the presence of moisture in the wood, which will not permit the cement to adhere properly. Often the surface will appear dry, but water, which has usually soaked deeply into the grain, will continue

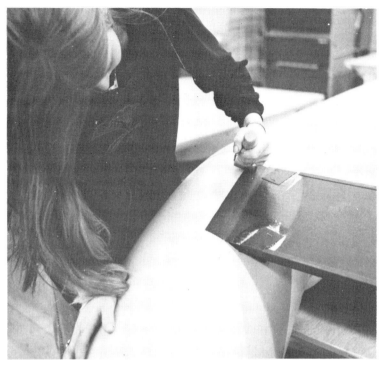

The thrust board is installed before the fabric bottom is added. With the bottom in place repairs to the thrust board can become difficult. Finding and repairing tears in the thrust board anchors is greatly simplified if they are detected and worked on before the damage becomes extensive. (Bonair Boats)

to work to the surface for a period of time. If this is the case, the only real answer is to expose the wooden area to the air, as best you can, and then give it an extended period of drying. Heat will help speed the process, but don't use so much that other parts of the hull are apt to suffer. Excess heat will also soften the adhesive in the seams.

The problem of cementing wood to the hull is often compounded by the inaccessibility of the area to be worked upon. This is especially true of the thrust boards, which sometimes begin to separate from their fabric mounts. The best and only worthwhile advice is to begin your thrust board repairs before the situation gets bad. Once you arrive at the point where the board is completely detached from the hull your difficulties are immeasurably increased. The trouble is that the thrust board connects to the hull at the base of the tube, just above the point where the bottom fabric joins, and the board is usually cemented, by fabric tabs, to both of these. Once the thrust board is detached from these anchoring points you are not only faced with the problem of recementing, but of realignment. This becomes a nightmare when you are working in cramped quarters, and your fabric surfaces are coated with contact cement.

Sometimes, with neoprene/Hypalon boats, the easiest solution is to turn the boat over, detach the bottom fabric from the hull tube, cement in the thrust board, and then reattach the bottom. With PVC boats this is not easy to do without cutting the fabric, so the only solution is to work slowly and carefully, head down, in the cramped quarters.

Doublers are strips of fabric which run along the inside of the hull and reinforce the joint where the fabric bottom joins the hull tubes. These strips are more vulnerable to chafing damage than most of the hull because the floorboards lay against them while the boat is running. Sand, gravel, shells can all work down into this area, and aided by the pressure of the boards, grind away at the fabric. Again, early detection and repair is the best cure. Normally the first indication that a problem exists will be the exposure of the threads of the underlying base fabric. At this point repairs are very simple. You can recoat the fabric with a number of layers of liquid neoprene (neoprene cement used in repairing wet suits works well), or liquid PVC, depending upon the type of material you are working with. You may have to repeat this process periodically, but it will serve to protect the area and prevent larger repairs later on.

If the doubler damage has gotten to the point where the fabric base is beginning to look badly frayed, or has worn through completely, then you must overlay the area with new material. Surface preparation consists of trimming away any fabric threads which might be hanging loosely, and then cleaning and buffing the area as you would for any normal patch.

Cement the lower half of the doubler in place first, without applying any adhesive to the upper half. This will permit you to accurately align the new strip along the bottom without the upper half touching and sticking. The doubler also makes a sharp bend where it transitions from the floor fabric to the tube. Cementing one side at a time makes it easier to force the material back into this tight corner with a screwdriver or similar tool. If you have applied cement to the entire doubler strip it is almost impossible to do this.

Waxed paper can be quite helpful when you have applied cement to a large area which must then be aligned. Slip the paper between the two pieces of prepared fabric, line things up, and then join the parts as you gradually slip out the paper. I mention this technique here, because it is frequently used on doubler repairs where you often work with long strips of prepared material. The same "waxed paper" procedure is useful when you are doing any large cementing job.

If you develop holes in the fabric bottom, these should be patched from the inside where the patches are more protected. With small holes this is normally all that is required, but if larger rips occur an additional exterior patch should be applied. Even though the bottom fabric is not subjected to the strain of internal air pressure as the hull tubes are, the material is still under considerable stress as the boat pounds through the water. The extra patching material on larger holes will greatly reinforce the torn area.

The base of the transom is an area which is very vulnerable and is frequently damaged. Impact with rocks, driftwood, and other hard objects crush the fabric against the non-yielding wood. For a time individual patches can be used to cover the damaged area and prevent water leaks, but as the boat becomes older the damaged area may become too large for this to be effective. At this point you should span the entire transom base with new fabric. If the keel strip (the strip of thicker material which normally runs the length of the keel) is intact at the transom, leave it in place and run your repair strips up to it on either side. If the keel has been torn off at the transom base, span the area with new fabric, and lay a new keel piece on top (or build one up with successive layers of fabric).

To be effective the transom patch should be at least twice as wide as the transom is thick, and must extend sufficiently far forward to find good solid holding ground for cementing. The patch should span the boat, at least far enough to port and starboard so that the damaged area is covered with about two inches to spare. On the outboard ends be certain to round off the corners to insure better adhesion to the bottom material.

If you find that your sportboat is subjected to more than the normal amount of abuse along the transom base, it will pay you to reinforce the area with metal strips. Stainless steel or brass are the best metals to use for this. If you use stainless you will provide sufficient protection if your metal is 1/64th of an inch in thickness. Brass, being softer, should be about twice this. Cut the metal, in width, so that it is about an eighth of an inch wider than the transom is thick and in length so that it runs from either side of the keel strip to about an inch inboard of the pontoon (provided that there is at least an inch-and-a-half of solid wood backing at this point). Of course, the edges of the metal should be ground-down so that there are no burrs to damage the fabric, and the corners should be rounded for the same reason.

When you position the metal on the transom do it so that the after edge is flush with the back of the boat. This will let the forward edge project just a bit ahead of the wood to give it added protection on impact.

The metal strip should be fastened at roughly 4-to-6-inch intervals, depending on the curvature of the bottom. The greater the curve, the closer the fastenings. Adjust the spacing so that the first and last fasteners are set about an inch inboard from the ends of the metal strip.

Use oval or round-headed screws about an inch in length. Oval is preferable, and should be countersunk so as to minimize the possibility of projecting edges which might catch debris. Nails can be used, but they don't work nearly as well as screws because there is very little holding power in edge-nailed plywood, from which almost all transoms are made.

Whatever type of fastenings you use, the metal in them should be compatible with that of the protective strip in order to minimize the corrosive effects of marine electrolysis. This occurs when dissimilar metals come in contact with one another in sea water.

Repaired inflatables are always suspect when they are returned to the marketplace for resale. You will have to prove to the new owner that what you have accomplished will be permanent and will not detract from the boat's performance. The price you get will be negotiable depending upon the number of patches, their condition and appearance. If you have done a workmanlike job there should be little reason to reduce your asking price. Neatly cut patches with rounded corners, proper cementing, and a thorough clean-up, will bring you more enjoyment and confidence when you use the boat, and more money when you sell it.

CLEANING — Sooner or later all inflatables become soiled when in use. The list of different soiling agents is practically endless, and this is closely matched by the number of products on the market which claim to be able to remove them. Most of these will work just as well on your boat as they do in the kitchen, and there is no point in trying to itemize all of the possible combinations. Common sense will be your best guide here. Always try any new cleaning agent on a separate piece of hull fabric before actually using it on your boat. Avoid harsh abrasives since these can damage the fabric if applied too vigorously. Strong solvents should be used sparingly, and with caution, since some of these will attack the fabric and others are able to weaken the cement in your seams and patches.

Beyond these general precautions there are a few specific hints which may be helpful in cleaning. Again, try them with caution the first time around since there are so many different fabrics on the market and some may disagree with these recommendations.

Tar and heavy grease clumps usually dissolve quickly (although they may leave a stain) if rubbed down with vegetable oil such as you use in cooking. This works well on diving and surfing wet suits too, in case you happen to be in the water after an oil spill.

Rust stains can sometimes be a problem when someone has inadvertently left a piece of raw iron sitting on the hull fabric. Normal detergents and other regular cleaning agents don't seem to lift these marks, but one or two light applications of "Rustbuster", a commercial compound made of alcohol and phosphoric acid, will bleach them right out. Wash the area with soap and water when the job is completed.

Marine growth can form on the bottom of your hull if your boat is left in the water for any extended period of time. Not just grass, but heavy stuff like barnacles will adhere to the fabric. Prevention is the best cure, which means hauling your boat out of the water periodically and giving it a good scrubbing. But if you have failed to do this, and your boat bottom has become an undersea garden and zoo, the cleaning process becomes a bit more drastic.

Remove the boat from the water and give it a good pressure wash with a fresh water hose. This will knock off a lot of the grass and many of the loose critters. Then slowly work over the bottom with a broad and dull putty knife with corners which have been ground round. If you have barnacles chip off the tops and leave their bases for later. Scrub off the remaining vegetation with kitchen cleanser, using a stiff bristle brush or some other type of scrubber (the 3M brand "Grill and Garage Scrubber", which comes with a built on handle is excellent for this). Once the hull is reasonably clean you can attack the remaining bits of barnacle shell using a solution of muriatic acid which will burn off the calcium deposits rather quickly. CAUTION: MURIATIC ACID WILL MELT NYLON, SO DO NOT USE IT IF THERE ARE CHAFED AREAS WHERE THE NYLON IS EXPOSED. The fumes from acid treatment are very acrid, so work outdoors and remain upwind. Finally, rinse the entire boat with fresh water to rid it of all the remaining acid. Remember, acid burns skin, eats away at clothes, and attacks metal fittings. Use it with sensible care to avoid these complications.

SURFACE COATINGS — If your boat remains dull and unenthusiastic looking even after it has received a good scrubbing, try spraying it down with a product called Armor All. This liquid coating is a chemical compound of highly resistant polymers, which penetrate, intertwine and combine with the polymer molecules in the hull fabric. This action is designed to protect the material from the destructive effects of ozone, ultraviolet rays and oxygen; but it also imparts a beautiful, "fresh from the factory", sheen to the surface. An Armor All treatment is worth doing once a season just for the protection it imparts, but it is also worth doing any time you want your boat to look good. Treated surfaces also tend to remain cleaner, since Armor All rejects clinging dirt. The only negative consideration when using Armor All is that a freshly treated surface will require a bit more preparation before a patch can be applied. All of the protectant material must be removed before the cement will properly adhere. A good scrubbing with soap and water, and then a thorough wash with acetone will be necessary, and then the surface should be buffed with sandpaper. Be careful, also, that you do not recontaminate the surface by touching nearby treated areas and then bringing the Armor All back on your fingertips.

Silicone spray is another liquid which will put a good luster on an otherwise drab looking hull. It also works quite well as a lubricant to make your floorboards slide in more easily. This substance must also be removed before attempting any repairs.

PAINTING THE HULL — In certain cases inflatable hulls can be repainted in order to restore them to a near-original appearance. Don't attempt to do this unless you have compatible paint. It must be formulated to apply to your particular type of fabric surface. Standard paints and enamels will not work. They will not cling to the fabric surface, and they cannot cope with the constant stretching, contraction and flexing which inflatable hulls undergo. As a result the paint will begin to flake off almost as soon as it is applied, and the boat will look far worse than if it had not been painted at all.

There are several companies who make paints which can be used on inflatable boats.

The Bonair Boat Company has developed a special liquid coating for use on their PVC impregnated hulls. This is a polyurethane system with good adhesion and toughness that exceeds that of the original skin. This polyurethane coating is similar to the adhesive used to construct the boats, and they have achieved excellent results with it.

Some of the canned vinyl paints will also work on PVC hulls. These are mostly made for refinishing vinyl upholstery, and in most cases they have an alkyd resin base which is not as good as the polyurethane coating which Bonair markets. Under certain circumstances the alkyd based paints will crack and peel, so it is advisable to pre-test any paint product which you intend to use, in order to avoid later difficulties.

Special coatings are also available for both Hypalon and neoprene boats. Two companies seem to dominate the market here, and they are both located in Seattle, Washington. Gaco Western, Incorporated, advertises coating materials for both Hypalon and neoprene; and Pacific Marine Development produces a Hypalon paint which they retail both through Zodiac of North America and directly through dealers. The products of both companies have a longer curing time than Bonair paint, and require at least a week to completely dry. During this period your boat should remain inflated to prevent the uncured surfaces from sticking together. If the boat must be deflated prior to that time talc or corn starch should be liberally applied to the entire surface.

Paints which have been applied to an inflatable hull will rarely have as good adhesion as the original factory coating. This may be a source of trouble if a patch is applied directly to the new coating. The patching adhesive may adhere to the paint, but under stress the paint may not adhere to the hull. If you must repair a boat which has been painted, it is essential that you remove the new surface coating before the patch is applied.

MOUNTING REGISTRATION NUMBERS — If your boat will be used with either motor or sail, the U.S. Coast Guard, and the various states, require that it be registered and display an identifying number. Theoretically these numbers must be mounted on the forward third of the boat, and be securely fastened to it. In practice, with inflatables, this can sometimes pose a problem. Ordinary stick-on letters and numbers will not stay in place because of the expansion and contraction of the hull. Normal paints won't either, for the same reason. This means that we must either use the somewhat expensive and slightly hard to get paints mentioned in the foregoing chapters, or use dyes, or mount your numbers on special boards which you then hang on your hull. All three of these solutions have been tried and work.

It is appropriate to mention one additional elastic paint which is available, and which has the advantage of drying very quickly. This is Vulcabond, which is manufactured by the Stabond Corporation in Gardena, California. This paint is produced in a variety of colors, it is a bit expensive, and requires special thinners; but it drys in minutes, and is very indelible. The trouble is that it has a short shelf life, so most dealers do not stock it, if they know about it at all. If your dealer does not have this paint and you still wish to use it you might contact the Stabond Corporation.

Black dyes are available in the form of the standard felt-tipped pens which are now a common item in retail stores. Choose one with a broad, quarter inch tip, and be certain that the label indicates that it is waterproof. Pens of this sort work quite well, but they are only semi-permanent. They tend to fade after about six months of exposure, and they can be removed by acetone and other solvents. Applying two or three coats will help to extend the life of your markings.

These can provide you with an easy and inexpensive way to apply your letters and numbers.

If you put your letters and numbers on the bow with paint or dye, you will still be faced with the problem of positioning the annual sticker, if your state issues one. If you merely press it on to the hull, in accordance with directions, it will fall off in short order. Cementing the sticker to the hull works sometimes, but this is time consuming and messy, and is still not guaranteed. Probably the best solution is to apply the sticker to some wooden or metal part of the boat, where it will cling properly and still be available for inspection if required. This could be the transom or motor bracket, perhaps a seat, or even the mast, if you have a sailboat. Placing the sticker in a remote location, away from your assigned serial number is not technically legal, but the logic of the argument should make it acceptable to the authorities.

The final solution to displaying your registration numbers is to mount them on boards, and hang these somewhere on your hull. Several companies make special plastic pieces for this express purpose, and these are generally available in marine supply houses. You can attach these number boards to your boat in a variety of ways. The simplest procedure is to tie them to the safety lines along the sides of the boat. A better solution is to cement "D" rings to the bow of your boat, and tie your boards to these. Mount the rings so that they are at either end of the boards, rather than at the top, and this will prevent the boards from flapping as you run through the water.

AVOIDING THEFT — Theft is the biggest problem which the inflatable owner has to face. Good inflatables are expensive, hard to identify, and can be compactly hidden away in the trunk of a car. Next to jewels and currency they are probably the perfect swipe. The question is, what can you do to avoid or minimize your exposure to loss? Aside from exercising common sense and normal vigilance, there are a few additional measures which may be of help.

The very first thing you should do is copy down your serial

number, so that if the boat is stolen you will have some way to accurately report the theft and identify the article if returned. In the event that your boat is not returned, but sold and reregistered by some unsuspecting new owner, your serial number will probably appear on the computer tapes and alert the authorities.

Theft avoidance and recovery is another good argument for the use of indelible paint, like Vulcabond, when mounting your registration numbers. If the boat is stolen and resold in your state the new owner will not be able to obtain a current sticker once the old one expires.

So much for passive measures. These are very necessary, but they should be augmented by other deterrents. The most obvious of these is to securely lock the boat up whenever it is not in use. If you store your boat deflated, keep the bags locked in a secure building, and try not to advertise the location to the neighborhood. If you keep the boat inflated then try to keep it in the garage, or if there is no room there, put it in your back yard or well up into the driveway. Boats which are kept on trailers should be chained in place, and the trailer should also be secured so that it can't be rolled away while you sleep.

A little ingenuity is required so that you can securely connect a chain or cable to an inflatable. Handles and "D" rings are not good points of attachment. It is too easy to cut these free and walk off with the boat. You must have some really solid and hard-to-cut fitting on the boat, and run your chain or cable to this. On boats with integral transoms, these offer the best possiblility. Bore about a one inch diameter hole through the wood to the right or left of the engine mounting location, and about an inch or so down from the top. The hole should be large enough so that you can pass your chain links or cable ends through and fasten them with a lock.

On boats without a transom the problem is somewhat more complicated. Sometimes the mount for the outboard bracket can be used since these are often quite sturdy. But this is by no means universal. If you have a neoprene/Hypalon boat, the best arrangement is to cement on one of the special anti-theft fittings manufactured by the Avon boat company.

These consist of heavy molded rubber fittings, which surround a hollow bronze cylinder. This unit is cemented to the hull of your boat, and provides you with a good solid anchor for your chain or cable. It may be possible to cut through the heavy rubber and release the bronze insert, but this is very unlikely without a very sharp knife and considerable spare time.

The chain or cable you use is as important as the strength of the point of connection on the boat, and so is the lock. If any of these are weak, then so is the entire system. If you use chain, use one which has good heavy case-hardened steel links. If these are galvanized to prevent rust, so much the

Some type of anti-theft device is excellent insurance when your boat must be left unattended. This heavy duty fitting made by Avon Inflatables can be cemented to the hull pontoon of neoprene and neoprene/Hypalon boats and provides a secure connection for lock and chain. (Avon Inflatables Limited)

better. The links should be heavy enough so that a hack saw or file will take an excessively long time to cut through. The same standards apply to cable. Buy one which is heavy, and preferably plastic coated so that you do not have to worry about chafe, or punctures caused by broken wire strands.

Locks always pose a problem, especially if used around salt water where corrosion can exact a heavy toll. Good brass locks, with case-hardened steel hasps, are the only answer; and even these must be well and continuously lubricated. Brass locks with brass hasps should be avoided. These offer very little protection, since brass is too soft to withstand any kind of serious cutting tool.

No anti-theft system is infallible, and this is one of the reasons why we have insurance companies. You should have insurance for liability protection in any event, and the policy should also protect you against the loss of your boat by theft or other forms of disaster. In some cases your boat may already be covered under one of your other policies, but if this is not the case you may be able to add a rider to provide coverage for a small additional sum. Check with your insurance agent on this. Small craft insurance is not usually expensive, and the protection it affords is well worth the cost.

Chapter 5

Hints for Better Boating

As with all boats, inflatables have characteristics which are unique to their breed. Their light, buoyant hulls give them a personality of their own which is unlike that of a hard boat in many ways. For this reason you must reorient your thinking if you wish to get optimum performance out of your inflatable. Even though you must make allowances for the softer, bouncier hull, you should still be able to obtain far better performance from an air filled boat than you would from a like-sized rigid hull. The secret lies in your knowledge of correct handling technique.

LOADING — No matter how buoyant or how stable, any boat can be improperly loaded to the point where its performance will suffer. If the boat is to glide efficiently and smoothly through the water, the weight of equipment and passengers must be balanced both fore and aft and from side to side. As a rule, the problem of balance does not become critical until the upper range of payload weight is reached, so long as the boat is running at full inflation pressure. The trouble is that under-inflated boats seem to be the rule rather than the exception, and the effects of poor loading are compounded as the boat becomes softer.

Weight distribution athwartships, which has always been the bane of the small hard boat skipper, is far less of a problem to the inflatable. A lateral weight shift which would tip over a hard boat is hardly noticeable to the owner of an inflatable. Nevertheless, some unbalanced drag will result, and this will increase fuel consumption and reduce top end speed.

Fore and aft loading is probably the most critical determination. Excessive weight too far forward will cause the hull to bend and deform, and greatly reduces performance because of lost hydrodynamic efficiency. Conversely, the placement of weight too far aft can aggravate the tendency of the light hull to lift its nose when headed into a strong wind, or when sudden large bursts of power are applied to the outboard.

Ideally, the weightload should be balanced on the centerline of the hull, and the center mass should ride somewhat aft of the mid-point of the boat. When the boat is light this may require you to move the fuel tank and adjust your own seating position. When it is heavily loaded it may be best to divide your cargo into light and heavy items and arrange them accordingly. Absolute precision is not necessary in loading because the floorboards will compensate for small errors (weight distribution is one of their functions). What you must avoid are extremes in either direction.

SEATING — "Where do I sit?" This is one of the first questions which most people ask when confronted with an inflatable. Many inflatables do not come equipped with conventional seats as standard equipment, and the buyer is left to his own devices when the time comes to use the boat. But this is not wholly true. Many people find that the pontoons which form the hull double quite nicely as seats, and it is quite common practice to use them for this. One person sitting on the side will not noticeably off-balance the boat, and it permits utilization of space which would otherwise be wasted. Most manufacturers anticipate that you will do this, and provide hand hold safety lines along the tubes for this purpose. The tubes should not be used for seating when operating in rough water or when high speed turns will be executed because of the danger of being thrown off the boat backwards. For these situations other seating arrangements should be investigated. Most inflatable boat retailers have a variety of seat types available as accessory items, and these are discussed in the following chapter which covers accessories and equipment. However, with a little imagination it is not difficult to come up with your own perfectly adequate seating method. If your boat has a rigid or semi-rigid floor it is perfectly acceptable to sit on this and use the buoyancy tubes as a backrest. Small cooler chests also work well provided you take steps to prevent hull chafing from exposed handles, latches or other sharp protuberances. If you keep it simple almost any seating device will work well provided that it is strong enough to support your weight as the boat bounces in rough water, and has a base which is wide enough to prevent tipping.

ROWING THE BOAT — The reputation of the inflatable as a rowboat is not one of its strong points. Not that it won't row, because it will; it is just that it won't row as well as its hard neighbor. The main problem is that inflatables lack weight, and lacking weight they do not have the momentum to continue sliding forward with a smooth movement between strokes. This situation is not helped by the generally snubby nose, shallow draft and low freeboard. The snubby nose gives them less than an optimum water entry, and the shallow draft adds poor tracking ability and leaves the boat more susceptible to wind-induced drift. Finally, the low freeboard makes the lot of the oarsman more difficult by positioning the oars closer to the water which places them in a less efficient pulling position. If you add to these basic difficulties the fact that most people underinflate their boats to the point where the oar mounts lack a firm base and roll downward and backward with every stroke, you can begin to understand why the inflatable has less than a superior reputation as a pulling boat.

Fortunately there are some ways to improve the situation. Begin by changing your rowing technique. Use short choppy strokes, or short alternating left and right strokes. The short strokes keep the boat moving through the water, and their frequency permits you to keep the boat more closely on its track.

Keeping a full charge of air in the hull will firm up the oarlocks so that you have something solid to pull against. A tightly inflated boat will also minimize pontoon deformity where passengers are sitting and aid in streamlining the hull.

For the really addicted oarsman, it is even possible (usually) to raise the oarlock position one or two inches by a bit of judicious jury rigging, using the existing oarlock mount as a base. The Avon type raised rubber oarlock is especially easy to modify by sandwiching it between two pieces of wood

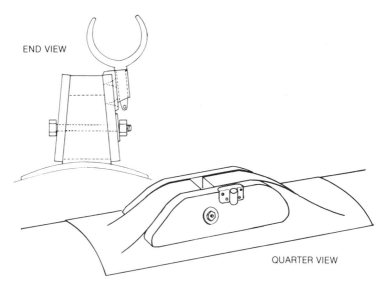

Technique for converting a molded rubber oarlock
to accomodate standard metal oarlocks
and to raise them to a more comfortable rowing position.

which are held in place by a bolt running through the old oarlock hole. With the wood firmly positioned you can mount a conventional oarlock socket to the outer piece which will effectively raise your oars a few inches. With just a little thought, and a bit of wood, fabric and cement, it is possible to modify most inflatables on the market in the same way.

Windage is another problem which exists with inflatables, especially with the flat bottomed dinghies which can skitter sideways pretty rapidly in a stiff breeze. Usually this is more of an annoyance than a problem unless there are aggravating circumstances, like very high winds or a lost or broken oar. Recognizing that this possibility always exists, it is a good idea to keep a sea anchor and signalling devices handy, especially when operating where there are offshore winds. This advice is not confined to inflatables. Any boat which becomes disabled is in danger of being blown out to sea unless quick action is taken. Always request assistance from any passing boat, no matter how embarrassing it may seem, and lacking that, take any action which will slow down the drift and/or get you back to safety. Substitutes for sea anchors can be rigged by tying oars, oar pieces, pants, shirts, buckets, etc. to the bow painter. Filling the boat with water will cut down the drift (inflatables will still float full of water) and let you sit on the bow with your remaining oar and paddle in, stroking first on one side and then on the other. If the water is warm and you are a competent swimmer shed your extra clothes and hop in the water. It takes very little effort to tow an inflatable by the bow line or handle if you use a good side stroke.

In view of the foregoing discussion, I think it is important to give some consideration to the problem of jointed oars. Most manufacturers of inflatable boats supply oars which come apart for stowage with the inflatable boat. There is no question that this is convenient, but jointed oars should always be treated with some degree of suspicion. No matter how well they are made, the center joint will always be a weak point. At the connecting point the oar has been turned down to permit the fitting of the interconnecting metal sleeves. These are normally held in place by screws, nails or pins which further weaken the wood. If there is any play in the joint, which is usual, this aggravates the problem by multiplying the stresses as the blade flops back and forth. Jointed oars should raise a flag of caution in the mind of the wise boatman, and a spare oar is an intelligent addition to your onboard equipment.

OPERATING UNDER POWER — An outboard is unquestionably the best and easiest way to propel an inflatable boat. Even the smallest putt-putt will push along a very respectable sized inflatable, and the addition of just a few horsepower on a sportboat will result in rather amazing performance. Here again, efficiency falls off quickly if the boat is run under-inflated. And, as we mentioned in Chapter 3, the maximum recommended engine size should not be exceeded for a number of reasons.

There is no particular trick to operating a dinghy under power. Hang the engine on the motor bracket, run a safety line to some other secure part of the boat in case the bracket or the motor should disconnect from the mounts, start her up and away you go. Check the engine position while the boat is running. If the shaft is not vertical try to determine the cause and correct it to improve efficiency. First, be sure that the boat is tightly inflated. If it is not, the hull will bend as power is applied, and you not only lose efficiency, but risk dunking your power head as well. If it turns out that your hull is tight, then it may be that your motor bracket is poorly positioned or the distribution of weight in the boat has made it so. Most engines have a tilt adjustment which will quickly improve the situation.

Soft bottomed dinghies are not planing hulls, so their top speed is necessarily limited. With a properly adjusted modest engine, and a normal load of passengers and cargo, most of them will chug along at a good two or three knots, and this is adequate for their intended use.

High-speed operations in inflatable boats is a whole new ball game. Sportboats are designed to plane over the water. That is, they obtain a significant portion of their weight carrying capability by interaction of the hull with the surface of the water. In this way drag is greatly reduced, and the biggest limiting factor to attainable speed is the power being delivered by the engine. Note that the hull is designed specifically so that it will plane. Dinghy and river boat hulls are not designed to plane, and the addition of larger amounts of power will have only negligible effect on the top speed which they can attain.

Getting your sportboat into a planing situation is a simple matter if you have sufficient power. As you add throttle the boat will begin moving forward and you will probably feel the bow begin to rise out of the water. This will continue for only a short time, at which point the bow will drop and the boat will pick up speed very rapidly. Once the boat is planing, power can be reduced without notable loss of speed. Usually it is a good idea to reduce power until you hear a distinct change in RPM. Operating at less than full throttle is better for the engine, and will greatly reduce the amount of fuel that it consumes.

You must combine good judgment and a bit of caution with powerful engines and high speed. With inflatables it is possible to exceed safe operating limits with many of the boat and motor combinations on the market today. As a rule it is not the boat which suffers, but the passengers. Inflatables go over waves rather than through them. At high speeds it is not unusual for boats to become airborne as they launch from the top of a wave, and the impact with the wave beyond can cause passengers and cargo to fly about, often with injurious results.

Unfortunately, planing operations require that the boat maintain some reasonable speed or the plane will be lost, and at speed, waves of any kind can be bothersome. Short choppy seas are unquestionably the worst to encounter. This is because of their greater frequency, and because their short abrupt sides do not give the hull a chance to conform to their shape. However, even large waves can sometimes become a problem at high speed, particularly when taken head on.

If you must go directly into the waves while running at high speed, and things become too jarring, the easiest solution is to reduce power until some degree of comfort is regained. Alternately, if you are able to take the waves on the quarter (that is, at an angle), you can often ameliorate the problem to some extent, and still run at your normal power setting. It is not considered bad form in an inflatable to tack back and forth in really choppy seas when you must go directly upwind. This may lengthen the trip, but it will smooth out the ride.

Running parallel to the waves is the least jarring condition, and can often be accomplished without reduction in power. As always, this must be tempered with judgment and a sharp eye, particularly where the seas are steep and white caps are breaking. It is a sickening feeling to be sliding down a waveface sideways, just as it is cresting over at the top. In such a situation it is incumbent on the helmsman to keep the boat running in the trough, or just slightly up the back of the wave ahead.

If the waves are large, running down-wave, either directly or at an angle, can be an interesting experience. On the forward slope of the wave the boat will pick up momentum and begin surfing downward, often with an attendant whine from the engine as the RPM increases. When the boat reaches the bottom of the trough and begins to make an upward transition, you will see the hull bend as the buoyancy of the bow works to counter the weight of cargo and passengers. This is where the underinflated hull begins to get in trouble. When properly inflated the hull may bend, but this will stop very quickly and without damage to the woodwork. However, if the boat is underinflated the bending can reach excessive proportions, and the strain will be transmitted to the more vulnerable and less resilient floorboards and stringers.

The motion of open water is difficult to describe, except to say that it is irregular. A good hand at the helm will learn to look ahead and anticipate the effect of the individual waves. Constant slight variations in throttle and heading can minimize the effect of most of these, while still maintaining good forward speed and overall direction of movement.

When a turn is executed on a properly balanced conventional boat the inside rail drops and the boat banks into it.

This is not the case with inflatables. They would like to do this, but the buoyancy of the inner tube prevents it. The end result is an almost flat turn. If the turn is a rapid one at high speed, the resultant centrifugal force on passengers and cargo can often be extreme, and persons sitting on the outer pontoon are in very real danger of being thrown over the side and into the water. At the same time the centrifugal force is working on the boat as well, particularly the heavier after end, thus causing it to slip sideways as the turn progresses. It doesn't take a geometrician to calculate that a fallen passenger will become a probable target for the whirling propeller. High speed turns should be executed with care, and with a warning, if people are seated along the pontoons. If operating conditions are such that high speed turns may have to be executed without warning, then the safest move is to ask all passengers to sit on the deck until safe maneuvering is again possible.

High speed inflatables tend to make fast flat turns. Use caution if you have passengers sitting on the hull tubes. The resulting centrifugal force can be sufficient to roll them off the side. (Bonair Boats)

ANCHORING — Not every anchor is suitable for use with an inflatable. An anchor may hold well enough on the bottom, but its configuration may be such that it becomes a storage problem when on the boat. There are four considerations when choosing an anchor for an inflatable: weight, holding power, stowability (size) and chafing.

An anchor holds a boat firmly in place by its ability to dig into mud, sand or gravel, or to hook on to rocks or ledges. To do this efficiently it must be designed so that it will automatically fall into the digging or hooking position when it reaches the bottom. Many different designs have evolved over the years as mariners have searched for anchors with greater holding power, or less weight, or better stowage characteristics. In truth there is no "best" anchor, What is best depends on bottom conditions, boat type, weather conditions, and a host of other less tangible requirements.

What the inflatable owner should look for is an anchor which is light in weight, stows compactly, has a minimum number of sharp points and angles which can chafe fabric, and yet which will still hold securely once it rests on the bottom. In one pass this will eliminate some otherwise very fine anchors like the Danforth, Northill, and kedge, which all have projecting arms, large sharp flukes, or both. Small mushroom anchors will work under some conditions, but these lack real holding power unless they have been able to settle deeply into the mud or sand on the bottom. A small plow anchor would be a likely choice except for its cost, which is more than most people would be willing to pay to anchor an inflatable. In the final analysis a five or ten pound stockless "Navy" anchor is probably the best choice. The price is usually reasonable, the anchor is compact and does not have any truly sharp projecting points, and it holds fairly well under most conditions. Another decent alternative is the small folding anchor, like the Norwegian SAV or the U.S. made Squid. These anchors have four flukes which fold inward when not in use. This permits them to stow very compactly, and they are also light in weight. The disadvantages are that they cost more than the Navy anchor, and they don't have quite the same holding power because they are not able to dig into some bottoms as efficiently.

There is always controversy among inflatable owners over whether the anchor line should be attached directly to the anchor, or separated from it by a 10 or 15-foot shot of chain. Adding chain is the normal procedure on most boats. The chain serves two functions: it guards against chafing on the most vulnerable portion of the anchor line, i.e. the section nearest the anchor, which is almost always lying on and moving about the bottom; and its weight dampens the surge and insures that the pull of the anchor will be parallel to the bottom, which makes the anchor bite more deeply into the substrate. From the point of view of the inflatable owner these advantages may or may not outweigh the problems of extra weight, and the possibility of chafing as the chain is dragged against the hull tube on its way back into the boat. Inflatables are not heavy boats, so there is less momentum to them as the boat rides upward and backward on passing waves. The value of chain as a surge dampener is therefore reduced, and a horizontal pull on the anchor can be achieved by letting out enough scope on the anchor line (no less than three times the water depth, and more under severe wind and weather conditions). In the final analysis chain or no chain must be governed by individual preference and local conditions.

Your anchor line should have sufficient body to it so that it doesn't fall into a massive tangle as you haul in the anchor and drop it into the boat. You should also select line made of synthetic materials, like nylon and Dacron, in preference to natural fibers, like cotton and hemp, because of their greater strength and relative immunity to deterioration. One quarter inch nylon three strand laid line is a good choice for most applications. It has a very long life, high breaking strength, ties or splices easily, and is not particularly prone to tangle. Nylon "parachute" cord is bad news, primarily because of its propensity to fall into a jumbled snarl when wet. Polypropylene also has disadvantages. It is quite slick and springy so that it does not store compactly, and it does not hold knots well. It also floats, which almost insures that it

131

will become tangled in the prop if you try to run up to retrieve your anchor.

The easiest way to keep track of and transport your anchor is by carrying it in a small plastic bucket. The bucket will keep the anchor from drifting about the boat and coming in contact with the hull tubes, and the line can be coiled away, untangled, as it is retrieved. The bucket can also serve as the repository for a foot pump and hose, repair kit, and other small items which you may wish to carry.

TOWING — Because of their light weight and shallow draft, inflatables are not difficult to tow behind another boat. Your inflatable can be towed for short distances by the bow painter, but this is not recommended for more than occasional use, because of the strain on the bow fitting. If towing is to become a regular practice, it is advisable to install matching towing rings on each side of the bow to which the bridle is attached. The bridle distributes the weight of the tow more evenly, and permits the boat to swing astern more naturally to the action of wind and wave. If you must tow a

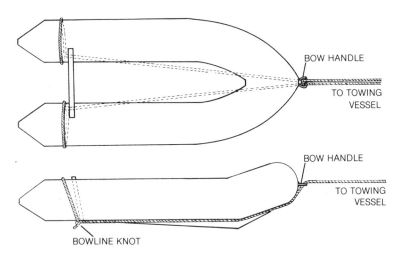

Technique for rigging a temporary towing bridle on a sportboat.

sportboat, for any distance, without towing rings, you can equalize the load by running the ends of a doubled over line through the bow handle and aft to the pontoon extensions behind the transom. Loop the lines, one to each side, over the tube extensions and tie them in place. This will balance the load without putting a direct strain on the bow handle.

Under normal circumstances the inflatable will tow more smoothly if it is snubbed fairly close astern. Some owners go so far as to pull the dinghy's bow up on the swim step, if they have one, and secure it there. If you prefer to keep your tow further astern, bring the towing boat up to speed (this should not exceed eight knots) and adjust the tow line so that the towed boat is riding in a comfortable position.

Needless to say, a towed boat is in a rather vulnerable situation, especially when high winds or seas are running. For this reason, valuable equipment should not be left aboard, nor should the engine be left in place. Additionally, it is always prudent to tie a second line to some other part of the tow as insurance in case the principal towing line should part. Towed boats can also ship water, so if your tow has drain plugs these should be left open. If the tow does not have drain plugs, stop periodically and check to see if water has accumulated. The additional weight of water in a towed boat can add considerable drag and severely strain the tow line and fittings.

It is preferable to tow a boat with its passengers removed. If this is not possible you should insist that each person wear a personal flotation device. Further, a watch should be posted to keep the tow under constant surveillance while the boat is underway.

DINGHIES AND TENDERS — There are many advantages to using the inflatable boat as a dinghy or tender. They are compact when folded, yet they are stable and have enormous capacity for their size. Their light weight makes them easy to launch and recover from a larger boat, while their soft sides offer a guarantee against collision damage. And an inflatable won't sink, even if swamped in the surf. With all of

Yachtsmen find inflatable dinghies hard to beat. They are light, easy to handle and stow in small packages, yet they have a large carrying capacity and don't damage the hull of other vessels when they impact against them. (Boston Whaler)

these qualities it is no wonder that more and more yachtsmen have turned to them as the answer to their small craft needs.

Even though many inflatables are purchased because of their compactness when deflated, there are times when it is desirable to carry the dinghy on board in the inflated condition. For short trips between anchorages this is sometimes done to expedite launching at the destination, and on long trips an inflated dinghy is a comforting device to have available for safety.

There are a number of acceptable techniques for on board storage of an inflated dinghy. For boats which have a swim step and sufficient beam, stowing the boat on its side on the (padded) step, and strongly trussed up against the transom, is an easy, effective and space saving solution.

Some very large boats sling their inflatables on davits. This works especially well if you are using a sportboat and wish to keep it inflated with the engine installed. The transom and the thrust board make handy points for attaching the necessary lifting eyes. Dinghies without transoms can be lifted by running straps around the boat near the bow and stern and connecting the lifting cable to these. If a more permanent arrangement is desired, large "D" rings can be cemented to the hull to which small bridles are attached. Dinghies on davits should be kept tightly inflated so that they don't droop (unseamanlike), and should have covers so that they shed rain and spray. If your dinghy has drain plugs these should be kept open.

If you wish to stow your boat on deck, but space is limited, it is perfectly acceptable to deflate one chamber, usually the bow, and fold this back over the other half. The half-inflated boat will still have sufficient buoyancy to support the crew in an emergency, and the flat chamber can be reinflated when they are safely on board.

Some manufacturers offer CO_2 inflating devices which can be used to blow up the boat in an emergency. If you should obtain one of these devices be careful to read the instructions, and to familiarize your crew with their operation. It is possible for some CO_2 units to overinflate the individual chambers if not properly monitored.

When CO_2 is used, the boat should not be tightly inflated, in order to allow for subsequent expansion of the very cold discharged gas. All compressed gases chill as they are released and expand, and the CO_2 is usually discharged into the hull at below freezing temperatures. This is one very good reason why CO_2 should not be used for everyday inflation, since the repeated discharge of below freezing gas can cause damage (freeze cracking) to the valve.

If you wish to go one step further it is possible, with a few modifications, to convert your dinghy into sort of pseudo-survival raft. Understand that this conversion is not intended to replace a proper self-contained survival raft, but merely to supplement it, since the dinghy will still lack many of the important survival features which the raft provides. Nevertheless, with the addition of CO_2 inflation, a canopy to provide shelter, a sea anchor to hold the bow into wind and seas and to minimize drift, and a waterproof kit full of survival gear, you will have one more place of refuge to climb into if the parent yacht should sink.

The canopy will consist of two parts: the canopy cover and the supports to keep it erect. The simplest way to design the canopy cover is to begin with a standard dinghy cover made to fit your boat. Have your canvas maker stitch an eighteen inch skirt along the lower edge. Add some grommet holes along the lower seam of the skirt so that you can secure it to the hull, and the canopy cover is made. The cover can still be used as a cover with the skirting material tucked underneath and inside the boat.

There are several ways in which to support the canopy. The oars are an obvious choice, and will work if the blades are crossed and tied together. By placing the oar handles inside, at the ends of the boat, they will form an inverted "V" upon which to drape the canopy cover. If you prefer something more sophisticated and roomy, try fabricating a supporting frame out of the rigid polypropylene tubes used by plumbers. This material is available in most hardware stores and is easy to work with, strong, and doesn't deteriorate in the marine environment. The tubing can be permanently bent by heating it, so that you can form a pair of arches tailored to the canopy shape. Pad the ends so that they don't chafe, and install some "D" rings on the inside of the hull to secure them to. Have some loops or ties sewn into the canopy cover to secure the frame, which will then be held erect by the canopy tie-downs along the top or side of the hull.

The Avon boat company offers a canopy kit for its dinghies which incorporates all of the necessary materials to do what we have just described. Additionally they can also install internally mounted twin CO_2 bottles which incorporate an overpressure relief valve. Both of these items should be available through your local dealer or by writing directly to one of the three U.S. importers.

Here are a few final thoughts before we leave the subject of inflatable dinghies. For the cruising sailor, dinghies make great bathtubs, with comfortable sides at just the right height to let you sit back and relax while you read a magazine or study the clouds. Inflatables are also useful for hauling large

Inflatable dinghies provide the kids with a lot of fun after a day at sea.
(Avon Inflatables Limited)

quantities of fresh water from the beach to your offshore yacht. Just lay a clean tarp on the inside of the hull and then fill the boat with fresh water. The dinghy won't sink, and can be towed, paddled or motored out to the larger vessel where it is pumped out. Inflatable dinghies can be inverted and placed between two yachts to act as a fender and very effective walkway, and if you have kids the boats provide a wonderful and safe diversion in the harbor after a long period at sea.

LAUNCHING AND RECOVERY IN SURF — When we speak of operations in the surf a word of caution is in order. Surf is a very variable condition, and for the inexperienced boater not something to be taken too lightly. Success in surf work is not learned simply by reading a book. Written advice helps by pointing out some of the basic techniques and problems, but to approach surf with confidence and safety this must be integrated with experience. Factors like wave set patterns, rip currents, beach gradients and tidal conditions all bear on the problem, and must be combined with good judgment on the part of the operator. Even with all the knowledge and skill you can acquire there are still going to be those days when it would be smarter to return home and spend the day in bed with a good book or someone.

Your normal ocean wave has been caused by the action of wind blowing on the surface of the water. The greater the wind, and the longer it blows, the greater the wave. Most of the waves you see on the beach have been caused by storm conditions somewhere in the ocean. The wind blows, the waves are formed, and they keep travelling until they reach some distant shore where they break. But the oceans are vast spaces, and at any given time in any one ocean there may be a number of storms generating waves of varying size and frequency. The waves from these individual storms travel outward from their source, and very often arrive at your beach simultaneously. Here they interact with one another, sometimes increasing each others height, and sometimes cancelling one another out. This is one of the major keys to success in surf work, because these high/low combinations lead to what we call "set patterns". If you look, you will almost always find distinct and timeable high and low patterns of waves rolling on to the beach. This knowledge will permit you to select the lower wave sets for your launch and recovery operations.

Rip currents are another standard surf feature which can be used to advantage when heading out to sca. Rips are caused by the piling of water on the beach through surf action. Excess water becomes trapped inside the surf zone, and as it accumulates it begins travelling left and right, along the beach, seeking a way to return to the sea. When one parcel of this water travelling one way meets a second parcel travelling the other, the shear mass combines to overwhelm the surf and rush back to the open ocean. At the point where this occurs the surf will always be less intense, and the velocity of this seaward bound current can be used to help transport your boat and shorten your exposure to the breaking waves.

Usually rips are easy to locate. As the water moves laterally along the beach it picks up all manner of sand and debris which it carries with it as it moves out to sea. As a result the area where the rip is moving will be discolored and carrying bits of flotsam, and the wave patterns will be lower and less distinct.

Beach gradient, or slope, will determine the characteristics of the surf you encounter. Steep beaches mean steep and fast breaking, often plunging, waves. Shallow beaches bring waves which break more slowly, and with far less violence. At times simply shifting your beach location will bring an appreciable change in surf characteristics. The same is true of tidal changes which often bring a distinctly different wave form as the tide comes in or recedes. It is here that experience and local knowledge are important, and here, too, where good judgment must play a part. If you look at the waves and have any doubts about launching through them, don't go.

Armed with the above knowledge you should be ready to try your first surf passage. Let us assume that on the first go you will be making the transit using your oars alone. Your boat is assembled, and blown up to proper operating pressure, and you have secured all loose equipment (packing it in watertight bags if required). You have selected your site to take best advantage of rips and beach gradient, and you have been timing your sets. You have found that you have roughly three minutes from the time the last large wave breaks until the first large wave comes crashing down in the following set. This does not mean that you will have a placid lake in between the big waves, but as a rule the waves you will encounter will be distinctly smaller in size. Set your oars in place so that they will be ready to use, watch for a set to pass, then quickly pull your boat into the water and walk it out keeping the bow pointed seaward. When you are about crotch deep, hop aboard, giving the boat a good push as you do. Now grab the oars and begin rowing. If all goes well you should be through the breaking surf, plowing your way seaward, well before the next set comes rolling in.

What do you do if you miscalculate? As a rule the best move is to keep going, and hope for the best. If you try to

Surf launching a powered sportboat can be easy if proper teamwork is used. With the boat afloat one member of the crew holds the bow into the waves while the other starts the engine and climbs aboard. Once the engine is warmed up and a period of low waves occurs the second crewman jumps aboard on command and the driver adds power. After the commitment to launch has been made the operator should keep the bow into the waves and head seaward. Speed should be consistent with safety so that surf transit time is minimized without causing the boat to become airborne as it passes over waves. All parties in the crew, especially those in the forward part of the boat, should be well braced and kneeling on padded cushions or lifejackets. (Lauren Hubbard)

turn back at this point the chances of being hit sideways and broaching are greatly increased. By continuing outbound and heading into the wave the probability of popping over the top are reasonably good, and you may be able to pass through the surf zone without further trouble. Even if things go wrong, if you have used some sort of good judgment regarding the maximum size of the waves which you will tackle, your wetting down should not be too extreme. The boat may fill, but it will still float, and you can drag it back up on the beach, bail it out, and give the surf another try.

With power, but without launching wheels, your problems are much the same. Your pattern of actions will be almost identical because the engine will have to be kept in the locked up position until you are in deep enough water to lower it without striking bottom. Since the engine can't be started until it is lowered, and since rapidly starting a cold engine can always be chancy, be prepared to finish the job with oars. If the engine does start on schedule, so much the better. Keep the bow pointed outbound and add throttle.

With launching wheels and power on a sportboat you can do wonderful things. The wheels raise the transom of the boat sufficiently so that the engine can be lowered into its normal operating position, and started, prior to the actual commitment to launch. The normal procedure is to walk the boat out into the water until the lower unit of the engine is submerged. Have someone hold the boat with the bow pointed seaward while you start the engine. If you have no partner start the engine in the shallows, where the boat is not being pushed about by the waves, and then rapidly pull it to deeper water so that cooling water can enter the intake of the engine. You can then wait for the lull between sets with the engine idling. When the lull finally comes, if you have a partner holding the bow of the boat, have him jump aboard before engaging the prop to avoid any possibility of injury. Once you and your passengers are aboard, shift into gear and apply power. If your engine is a large one, the passage may be bouncy as you run over the smaller incoming waves, but as compensation the trip will be a quick one. When you are well outside the surf zone, stop for a minute and remove the wheels.

With power the same rules apply once you have committed yourself. Don't change your mind and try to reverse course. It is always better to take a breaking wave bow-on than sideways, and this is especially true if you have an engine, or an engine and wheels, projecting below the boat. The addition of sideways drag from your appendages will increase the possibility of an overturn, and if your projecting parts strike the bottom with the force of a wave behind them they stand an excellent change of being heavily damaged.

The technique of returning to the beach through the surf will again differ depending on whether you are using engine power or oars.

If you are using oars, and the waves are spilling over, rather than plunging when they break, then you can pretty much row right in, letting the individual waves pick you up and surf you along. Even if the boat is pitched sideways in spilling surf it will rarely tip, especially if the passengers lean towards the breaking wave. But if the waves are steep, and breaking sharply, then you will have much better luck if you back the boat in, and pull toward the breaking waves as they occur. With large waves it is also helpful to stream a sea anchor. This will keep the bow into the waves, and keep them from pitching the boat shoreward, out of control.

If you are running the boat into the beach under power the problem is greatly simplified. As always, it helps to pick out your sets and utilize the low periods to make the passage, but this is not absolutely critical so long as you have sufficient power to move the boat along at the same velocity as the waves.

When you wish to make your run into the beach, circle offshore for a moment until you pick out a point of intended landing. Keep an eye on the wave motion, then when you are ready to make your run set the boat on the back of a wave and ride it in. If you do this correctly the wave will eventually be breaking right under the bow of the boat. This can be disconcerting, but keeping the boat well up on the back of a wave serves two functions: it keeps you in deeper water which

Returning through surf is easy provided you have sufficient power to ride in on the back of a breaking wave. (Don Hubbard)

permits you to run in under power for a longer time; and you stay well ahead of the wave behind, which gives you a moment longer to react once you cut the power in the shallows.

If you are running into a smooth beach, and your boat is equipped with wheels, keep the engine running until you actually touch down on the sand. The momentum of the boat will run you forward if it is aided by the push of the prop, and the wheels will usually raise the transom until it is clear, or nearly clear, of the water. This reduces the amount of impact area which the following waves will encounter, and keeps you from shipping a large amount of water over the transom.

If you are operating under power, without wheels, all of the initial procedures still apply, but depending on the beach gradient you may have to cut your power further out. This will greatly increase the likelihood of taking water over the stern, and it is more probable that the boat will broach in the shallows. Since you can expect this to happen at least fifty percent of the time, plan for it, and complete the operation in the following sequence: Cut the engine just before you feel that it will touch bottom, and quickly reach down and pull it into the up position. Lock it there. By this time the boat will begin to swing sideways, one way or the other. Jump out on the *seaward* side, and use the momentum of the boat to turn the bow into the oncoming waves. You can now let the boat ride into the beach on the whitewater, as you guide it in by the bow handle.

In the final analysis you are far more likely to be successful in surf work in the stable and buoyant inflatable than in any hard boat. If you should miscalculate, and your boat fills with water or overturns, it will still float and remain manageable, and there will be far less danger of injuring the occupants than there would be with a wood, metal or fiberglass hull.

TROUBLE ON THE WATER — No matter how carefully we operate there is always some possibility that the hull will be punctured while the boat is in use. That sudden hissing sound, and the sight of your hull deflating, can be a heart stopper. But that is precisely why inflatable boat hulls are chambered. One portion of the hull may change into a floppy mass of fabric (and even this rarely happens quickly), but at least you know that your boat won't sink. And usually, if you are operating under power, you will even be able to keep on motoring once you get things organized and under control.

The initial step in any emergency is to try and locate the leak so that you can slow down or stop the rate of loss of air pressure. If the hole is a small puncture, and it is inside the boat or above the waterline, you can simply put your thumb on it and keep it there while you run into shore. If the boat has softened appreciably while you are searching for the leak use your pump to add additional air. Wide strips of tape will sometimes work to stop the air leak once the pressure is somewhat reduced, but the adhesive is rarely strong enough to remain attached to the hull when the boat is at full pressure.

If the puncture is such that the air loss cannot be stopped, you must take whatever steps are necessary to save your equipment and to keep the interior of your boat reasonably dry. Even with a serious rip you should not expect the afflicted chamber to collapse immediately. Trapped air, and the support of the adjacent chambers, will usually keep the tube partially inflated while you organize for the crisis. Shift your cargo and passengers to an undamaged portion of the hull, and then, if the tube is settling uncomfortably low into the water, grasp it by the top and raise it to form a temporary side while you proceed.

If you are in a powered dinghy which has chambers fore and aft, and the forward chamber fails, pull the loose material aft to form a bulkhead, and continue on your way using your engine. If the failure is in the aft chamber you will have to stop the engine and retrieve it before it tucks under and is dunked. After you have rescued the engine, pull the

Even though all of the valves are open and the tubes deflated this sportboat is able to plane using a 20 H.P. engine. The hard keel on this boat helps to maintain its longitudinal rigidity. (Barron Sams, Novurania Inflatables)

146

deflated chamber forward (or if the leak is slow and the chamber has not noticeably deformed let it trail behind), and row or paddle to safety. Since it is not normal for dinghies to be operated at great distances from land or the parent boat, the consequences of a puncture are rarely likely to be serious.

Almost all sportboats are designed so that the engine will operate even though one, and often two, chambers are fully deflated. This is possible because of the stiffening and thrust transmitting effect of the floorboards and keel, coupled with the buoyancy of the residual air trapped in the damaged chamber(s). It is not unusual for the boat to be able to plane in this condition, with due consideration to sea state. If the return trip will be a long one, and the hole is not too large, it is prudent to continue adding air to the afflicted chamber using your pump, or any other source of air (scuba tanks). Shift cargo and passengers as necessary to keep the weight over the good chambers. This will place it/them in a safer and dryer location, and the reduced weight on the bad area will result in less air loss from the punctured chamber.

Truly disabling damage to a good inflatable is a rare thing. Sharks don't bite them, and unless you have a psychopath aboard, people don't intentionally stick knives and pins into them. Most damage, if it occurs, comes from internal chafe, which usually causes a small but controllable hole. Punctures from external impact are rare, but when these do occur the built-in safety features of the chambered hull come to your aid. On hard-shelled boats, high impact damage, which holes the hull, will mean swamping and clinging to an almost submerged boat. I'll take my chances on an inflatable any time.

RIGHTING AN OVERTURNED BOAT — What you do if the worst happens and the boat accidentally becomes inverted? Admittedly, it is rare for this to happen, but once in a while circumstances gang up and an inflatable will flip. The problem is, the boat will be just as stable upside down as it is right side up, and while the boat won't sink, you will probably be considerably happier if you can flip her back to her normal position and climb aboard.

Standing on the side of the inverted boat won't do it, UNLESS you attach a rope (or ropes, depending on the size of the boat and the help available) to the opposite pontoon and lean way back to overbalance the hull. Even then you may have to *throw* your weight outboard to gain sufficient momentum to break the initial suction; and you may also have to haul in on the line, hand over hand, as the boat begins to lift out of the water, to keep from falling into the drink before the job is done. If there is any wind your efforts will be aided if you can turn the boat broadside to it and stand on the lee (downwind) side. This way, once the upwind side of the boat clears the water the wind will assist in the lift.

SCUBA DIVING — One of the earliest groups in the United States to accept the inflatable boat were the divers. Scuba diving is a sport which requires a lot of heavy equipment, and a good diving boat must combine considerable weight carrying ability with super stability. The inflatable has both of these qualities in abundance, along with its other virtues.

For short trips almost any inflatable can be adapted for diving, even the soft bodied dinghies, and some canoes and kayaks. But for true utility as a diving platform the inflatable sportboat is the preeminent choice. The ability to mount a large engine gives it the power to quickly push its heavy cargo to the more distant locations, and the larger tube diameter adds buoyancy and stability while, at the same time, keeping the passengers and gear dryer. The sportboat also provides a solid decking of some sort, and this makes a much better platform for rigging equipment and suiting up.

The key to success in diving from any small boat is in organization — stowing your equipment so that it is accessible but orderly, and there is a lot of equipment to stow. One of the cardinal rules of diving is that you must dive with a partner, so this automatically means two or more complete sets of diving gear, plus whatever additional paraphernalia

Inflatables make superb diving platforms because of their super-stability and great capacity. Many Americans were first introduced to inflatables while watching Captain Jacques Cousteau and his adventurous crew on television. This photograph was taken during his whale expedition. Though the dictates of this particular operation required a moving boat, it is an extremely dangerous and unacceptable practice to be in or under the water in the proximity of an uncaged, whirling propellor. (Zodiac of North America)

each party carries along. In addition there must also be room for fuel, anchor, line, pump, and the usual personal flotation devices required by the U.S. Coast Guard (note that inflatable buoyancy compensators do not count as PFD's unless they have a label indicating Coast Guard approval for this purpose. At this writing, none do).

Stowing your diving tanks is the biggest problem because of their weight and size. It is usually best to stow tanks on their side, oriented in the athwartships direction. Locate them just aft of amidships, where they keep the hull in balance and yet receive a minimum of bounce. Chock them in place with weight belts, if you have them, and be certain that valves and tank boots stay clear of the sides of the boat where they may chafe. You can use the horizontal tanks as seats if you cover them with cushion type PFD's which are legal in boats under 16 feet in length. If you plan to carry more than one tank each on your diving trips then a tank rack, which transports the tanks in a vertical position, is a great space saving asset.

Equipment bags, which are light and usually don't contain much hardware, can be stowed forward, along with your other spare gear and boat equipment. Here is where using a bucket for your anchor and pump is valuable, since it keeps this equipment separated and readily accessible for use later on.

Bottom depth is always of importance to a diver, since deep dives result in a more rapid build up of potentially dangerous nitrogen in the system. Marking the anchor line with red paint or dye in ten foot increments gives you a handy way to determine how deep you will be going without having to carry a portable depth sounder.

Donning equipment is rarely difficult in an inflatable because you are not confined to the center of the boat.Sit somewhere along the side, where you are not crowded and can work comfortably. If there are more than two divers, part of the group can assist the others, and then get them into the water in order to make more room.

The trick to making a water entry is to get out of the boat without dragging sharp items, like buckles, knives or tank boots, across the hull tubes. Leave your speargun, or other sharp, bulky or vulnerable equipment in the boat, with your partner, or hang it off the transom on a lanyard, while you make your water entry. You can retrieve it after you are in the water when you have things under control.

There are several simple ways to get into the water from an inflatable. The easiest entry is the back roll. Check the water alongside to be certain there are no obstructions, then sit on the side, facing inboard, hold your face mask, and roll over backwards. A forward roll can be executed by placing one hand on the tube, and using it as a pivot to tumble into the water. Give a light spring with your knees as you go and you will hit the water about on your shoulders, with the tank absorbing the impact. Lastly, for the diver who just can't come to grips with forward and backward rolls, an effective and less violent water entry can be accomplished by laying face down on the tube and then rolling sideways into the water.

Your first stop underwater should be at the anchor, to see that it is holding properly and that the line is not chafing. There is rarely room for an additional passenger to sit and wait on a diving boat, and a dragging anchor can result in a long and tiring return swim.

When you have completed your dive, relocating your boat can sometimes be a problem. Your eye level is just an inch or so above water level, and if there is any swell running the relatively low lying boat may only appear now and then as it rides up and down. The solution to this problem is to mount your "Divers Down" flag on a fairly long mast attached to the transom. The thin fiberglass whip masts, which are sold in bicycle stores, are the ideal solution. They are slender, quite long, easy to mount, and virtually unbreakable.

Reentering an inflatable after a dive can be an easy operation. Take off your weight belt and drop it into the boat. Remove your tank, and hand it to your buddy, or buckle it to

Water-skiing poses no problem for sportboat owners who mount an engine of sufficient horsepower. (Zodiac of North America)

151

the safety line or lifting handles along the side of the hull. Deflate your buoyancy compensator, and leave your fins on. Place your hands on the top of the hull tube, press down, and give a powerful kick. This will propel you out of the water, and up on to the tube. One further kick will get you into the boat. The soft tubes do not chew into your ribs or bark your shins as you come over the sides, nor does the boat tip dramatically. These are some of the often overlooked features of inflatable boat diving.

If you are wearing a wet suit you will bring a lot of water aboard after each dive. This is where self-bailers are handy. If your boat does not have these, they can be installed very easily on most sportboats.

Spearfishermen must realize that the spines of many fish can puncture the fabric of hull tubes if they are dropped heavily against the sides. Catch bags should be set well toward the center of the boat, or placed in the anchor bucket for safekeeping.

WATER-SKIING — The mention of water skiing with an inflatable boat almost always generates an incredulous look. It never seems to occur to some people that a boat, is a boat, is a boat. You could water ski behind a wooden shoe if you could find one large enough and put a powerful engine on it. And an inflatable sportboat is a lot more sophisticated than a wooden shoe. In fact, any high speed inflatable with a powerful engine will perform extremely well as a water-ski boat, and a good many do.

Power, of course, is the key to performance, which means that you can forget about water-skiing behind your dinghy with the three horsepower Seagull engine. How much power do you need? Under average conditions, no less than twenty horsepower, though you may be able to get along with something slightly smaller if you will only be pulling children or very lightweight adults. In addition, the engine should be equipped with a propeller designed for pulling loads. Check with your dealer on this. As a general rule of thumb, a twenty horsepower engine on a twelve to fourteen foot inflatable will give you a boat and motor combination capable of pulling one average size person, on two skis, at about twenty miles per hour. Naturally, if water-skiing is going to be your major boating diversion, you will want to mount an engine capable of delivering 40, 50, or even greater horsepower. Larger engines permit fancy slalom skiing, and add the possiblity of pulling multiple numbers of skiers.

As we mentioned in Chapter 3, when you are in the process of selecting your boat and motor combination, you must decide, in advance, what you want the boat to do and how you want it to perform. Not every sportboat is capable of mounting an engine suitable for skiing, especially in the higher horsepower brackets. If skiing is going to be your game, carefully check into this before putting your money on the table.

Equipment requirements for skiing with an inflatable are identical to those needed with a hard boat. The tow-line should be attached to the transom with a "V" sling connected to towing eyes on either side of the engine. This helps to distribute the load evenly behind the boat, and it keeps the pull on the tow line centered. If your sportboat has no provisions for mounting a sling, you can bore two holes in the transom about an inch or two down from the top, and install a pair of ring bolts. The tow line will exert a lot of pressure on these fittings, so these should be backed with large washers to prevent damage to the wood. When the boat is to be deflated and rolled up for storage the towing eyes should be removed, or well padded, to prevent chafing the fabric hull.

When water-skiing with an inflatable there is a slightly different feel to both driver and skier. The inflatable makes flat turns, and has very little draft forward. To a minor extent this allows the boat to react to the actions of the skier. The boat may slew a bit, to right and left, as the skier maneuvers. This movement is usually insignificant, and the boat will remain fully under control at all times.

Retrieving a downed skier is a safe and painless business with an inflatable because of the soft and stable hull. Approach the individual from downwind, put the engine in neutral, and glide alongside. If you miscalculate and bounce against your swimmer there is no damage done, and if you have no bathing ladder and must pull him into the boat you can both put your weight on one side without danger.

Water-skiing is a wonderful and growing sport, and the inflatable is ideally suited to it. The economy of being able to ski behind an inflatable, using a smaller engine with its greater fuel economy, will continue to make the boats more and more attractive as the price of gasoline continues to climb.

SAILING — To many people, boating means sailing. In the inflatable business this was an area which the inflatable manufacturers neglected for many years. Zodiac, the French company, developed two sailing kits for their boats in the early 1960s. One of these was a very sophisticated sloop rig, and the other a smaller survival sail for use in emergencies. For one reason or another these were both discontinued, at least so far as North America was concerned, even though the two rigs appeared to be quite practical. But in later years many manufacturers have come to realize that consumer demand exists for sail-powered inflatables. As a result, many sailing rigs have appeared which will convert standard inflatables into sailboats, and some craft have been produced that are designed primarily for sailing.

How do inflatables sail? This, of course, depends on the rig, the boat, the sea state, the wind, and on the individual skipper. But in general they sail much like any other small craft, and they are steady sailers. Steady both in the sense that they are stable, and that they will move along nicely under most wind conditions.

Inflatables whose hulls are made of reinforced fabric, in general perform better as sailboats than those whose fabric is not reinforced. The reinforced fabric can be pumped to greater pressure, and is therefore stiffer, giving the boats better water entry characteristics. Reinforced fabric also flexes less, and consequently the hull has less drag.

Sailing inflatables are rarely as fast or maneuverable as

Several manufacturers offer optional kits to convert their boats to sail. Even though made of unreinforced fabric this Sevylor K-88 sportboat is able to perform well in strong winds and on choppy seas. Windage is controlled by leeboards. (Sevylor Inflatables)

hard boats of comparable style. This is because their blunt, rounded inflatable shape does not slice through the water as keenly, and because their lack of weight and momentum rounds them up into the wind more slowly when tacking. The weave of the fabric also decreases performance, to some extent, because of its friction with the water, as opposed to the slick, hard finishes on most sailboats.

Sideways slip is something which all sailboats must contend with, and in inflatables this is countered by the use of adjustable leeboards on either side. Leeboards substitute for keels and centerboards found on most hard sailboats. As their name implies, the lee, or downwind board is pushed down into the water, while its twin, on the opposite side, is raised to reduce drag.

Leeboards project some distance below the boat, and because they are able to swing, their position is adjustable within certain limits. Experiment with this. Inflatables are more effected by the wind than most hard hulls, and very often the leeboard in the full down position will be too far forward to counter the effects of the wind on the aft part of the hull. In this situation the boat will fight to round itself up into the wind. When this happens, if the board is swiveled somewhat further aft, the sailing characteristics should improve.

As mentioned earlier, tacking an inflatable is not the easiest thing to do. If the boat is already running close-hauled, and you wish to bring her about and go off on the opposite tack, it is very likely that she will come up into the wind, and stop right there. There is just not enough momentum in the light hull to permit her to swing clear through against an opposing wind. There are no guarantees here, but you will probably do better if you let the boat fall off on a beam reach, in order to pick up speed, before putting down the helm to bring her about. If your boat has a jib sail, let this run free as well, so as to reduce the wind resistance on the forward portion of the boat. When used in combination, the two foregoing tricks will usually bring you about. And if all else fails, you can always use a paddle or an oar to give the boat a small assist, purists to the contrary.

Inflatable sailboats do not tend to heel over nearly as much as hard boats. The stability of the pontoons is to thank for this. For this reason they make great learning boats for the new sailor. This is not to say they are tame, just less error prone. For the individual who enjoys sailing for sailing's sake, and who can use and appreciate the other unique features of the inflatable, they offer many advantages.

FISHING — Perhaps you wonder why this section has been added to this book — there is nothing earthshaking about fishing from an inflatable, it is done all the time. Nevertheless, newcomers to fabric boats often have legitimate questions and reservations about the safety of this practice, and they often wonder how you mount poles, arrange seating, store live bait, and solve other related problems. There are answers to all of these questions, and they are worth mentioning.

Inflatables make fine fishing boats. They are easy to launch even without launching ramps, engine requirements are minimal, and in most cases their super-stability permits stand up casting. (Boston Whaler, Inc.)

157

Unquestionably, some minor precautions should be taken when using fish hooks, knives and gaffs, around an inflatable. The same precautions apply when using these same items around a puncturable human being. If you sprinkle loose fish hooks around the boat, you are just as apt to get one in your foot as you are in the hull tube — the same with knives and gaffs. If your equipment is properly stowed, both your boating and your personal problems will be few.

If you use a gaff, this presents the biggest problem, because it is larger and harder to store. A large piece of cork, or Styrofoam, placed on the tip is a big help, or very often you can eliminate the problem altogether by substituting a net for the gaff.

Folding knives work just as well for cutting bait or gutting fish as sheath knives do, and they can be snapped shut when not in use.

Fishhooks! How many inflatable boats have not been sold because of the misbelief that fishhooks will spend the better part of their time punching holes in the skin? Does this ever happen? Rarely, and when it does the fault can almost always be traced to the operator. If you have a hook on a line and you pull it up with the fish on it, the fish usually protects the boat by burying the hook away, somewhere in his innards. If the hook comes up naked, then it usually has insufficient weight to it to do more than bounce off the rounded side of the boat. What can, and occasionally does, happen is that the hook inadvertently catches onto the slightly protruding lower edge of one of the seams or external patches. This, in itself, is usually harmless, and if you stop for a second and gently disengage the hook, nothing further will happen. However, if you see or feel the hook engage, and then haul in sharply, to try and break it loose, you are certain to have a puncture. The simplest answer to the hook-in-boat problem is to think about what you are doing as you reel in. Hold your rod tip outboard of the boat, and reel in until the hook clears the water. You can lift it inboard, above the hull tube, and avoid a snag. The same technique works with hand lines. Don't just drag them in across the side of the boat. Haul them in, hand over hand, and when the hook becomes visible, lift it up and over the tube.

If you are planning to fish from a sportboat, and wish to mount your rod so that you can troll, this is easy to do. Go to your marine supply house, and buy a pair of metal or plastic fishing rod holders. Mount these on the inside of the transom (with bolts and wing nuts, so that they can be easily removed when the boat is to be stowed), one on either side of the engine. Position them at about a forty five degree angle to the deck. This will position each rod tip and its trailing line well outboard of the hull tubes, and leave the rods easily accessible if you should get a strike.

If you wish to have a swivel seat, most marine supply houses stock, or can order, fiberglass seats which have backs, and which are mounted on sturdy, square pedestal bases. The pedestals are roughly 14 inches high and 18 inches square, so the whole unit will fit nicely amidships, and positions the seat at about the level of the pontoons. The seat can swivel 360 degrees, which makes it convenient to direct your cast in any direction, or to face aft and hold your pole while trolling. The seat base also allows for storage below, so the space is not wasted.

Your marine retailer can also supply a variety of other swiveling seats in different styles, and without bases, so that you can improvise your own pedestal. This might be a box housing your fuel tank, a cooler chest, or any similar arrangement.

If you plan to use live anchovies for bait you will have to provide them with a continuous supply of fresh water or they will use up the oxygen and die. There are live bait cages which can be towed astern, but these slow the boat considerably, and are not practical if you wish to fish some distance offshore. The problem is no different with a hard boat. If you want to travel to the fishing grounds at reasonable speed, and carry live bait, then you must carry a holding tank with circulating water. A full discussion of equipment of this type is contained in Chapter 6 (Equipment and Accessories) which follows.

Lest you suspect that fishing from an inflatable means confining yourself to small fish it is worth mentioning that one friend of the author regularly uses his 15 foot boat for shark fishing 8 to 10 miles off the California coast. There are also several instances where large billed fish have been taken from air-filled fabric boats. Thrilling, perhaps, but still possible.

HUNTING — Many of the features of the inflatable dovetail nicely with the requirements of the waterbird hunter. Because of its light weight, the fabric boat can be easily hauled to the water near the blind. Its minimum draft and buoyancy permits it to slip through marsh grass, and over shallows, which would bog down a heavier boat. The inflated tubes provide a soft and insulated seat for the sometimes long and cold wait for the birds; and stand-up shooting is possible, because of the inflatable's super-stability.

For the hunter who uses dogs for retrieving downed birds, dog-damage is no great danger while the animal is in the boat. The fabric on good boats has sufficient thickness and strength to withstand this kind of wear. However, some precautions should be taken when the dog returns to the boat with the catch, because some animals paw at the side of the boat in an attempt to reenter. Lead the dog alongside by the collar, and then lift him aboard parallel to the hull. Laying a towel, or a piece of canvas, on the hull tube at the point where the animal is brought aboard should be an additional safeguard.

For the hunter who wishes to camouflage his boat there are paints which are suitable for the purpose, as we mentioned earlier. The majority of the inflatables on the market are already neutral in color, which provides a good base for further creative effort. Netting and other camouflage materials can be added in the usual way.

My own choice for hunting is a twelve foot sportboat propelled by a modest engine. A boat of this size fits into most blinds, and the wooden decking provides insulation from the cold water and makes it easy to stand and move about. The use of a sportboat also permits traveling greater distances

Hunters find that inflatables make superb platforms. They are easy to launch, even without ramps or special facilities, they push through swamp grass and reeds easily, and their stability makes stand-up shooting a feasibility. (Novurania Inflatables)

161

Even inexpensive inflatables, like this kayak made of unreinforced PVC material, can provide a lot of whitewater adventure on moderate rivers when used with good judgement and proper safety equipment. (Sevylor Inflatables)

more rapidly, and the boat can be used for many other alternative purposes as well.

RIVER RUNNING — Not all inflatables are ideally suited to the special requirements of river running. Boats with wooden floorboards and hard transoms are too easily damaged because of the lack of give in the hard surfaces. Sportboats are occasionally used on rivers, but they are a poor choice. The same applies to catamaran hulls, whose separated units, with their connecting spars and other devices, are not stressed for the added forces of high velocity impact with river banks and rocks.

The proper river boat is the all-inflatable, in whatever form. Canoes, kayaks, dinghies, some sport-tenders like the Metzeler Aztek, Maya and Juca (which have inflated deck and removable transoms) and, of course, the large, heavy-duty riverboats themselves. Your selection and use of any one

Paddling a riverboat downstream requires both coordinated effort and individual initiative. River-running can be an exhilarating experience, but it is important that everyone on board wear proper safety equipment and be briefed on proper procedure if thrown into the turbulent water. (Campways Inflatable Boats)

of these will depend upon the type of river you plan to tackle, and its particular rate of flow at any given time.

It is essential to mention that river running, while it can be a beautiful, exhilarating experience, can sometimes be very hazardous, especially to those who are new at the business. It is not just a matter of being able to handle the boat. Just as importantly you must be able to recognize and anticipate critical situations before they occur, and understand the dangers they portend. You must be able to "read the river" by utilizing the often subtle signs which all of your senses will eventually learn to detect by experience.

At this writing, most major rivers have been charted by

knowledgeable people, and with just a little bit of pre-study you should be able to learn where the major trouble spots are likely to be, and how to avoid them. Books like WHITE-WATER RAFTING by William McGinnis, go into great, and very necessary, detail to explain all of the hazards which the river runner may have to face and the proper procedures which should be followed to negotiate each of these. When this information has been read and digested, then, and only then, should you make your first timid approach to this sport.

The true river boats are propelled by oars, or by paddlers who usually sit astride the hull tubes. If you wish to row your boat, then a rowing frame must be constructed and lashed to the tops of the hull tubes. This permits the operator to seat himself so that he is facing downriver, where he can watch the

The rowing frame permits the operator to face downriver and quickly maneuver the boat to avoid obstacles. (Avon Inflatables Limited)

water and maneuver the boat accordingly. He is in sole control of the craft, and the success of the passage will wholly depend on his ability. This is not so in paddled craft. Here each man must respond to the directions of the helmsman, and in many cases, to the situation as he, himself, sees it. Paddling a boat downriver involves the whole crew, and the chances for error are greater even though the mutual effort can add an extra share of enjoyment.

It is difficult to provide any definite outline of the equipment needed by an inflatable for river use. This is because of the seemingly endless number of variables in boats, numbers of people, type of river, length of trip, etc. However, there are certain items which every trip should include.

Aside from the boat itself, the propulsion equipment is of primary importance. Oars and paddles must be made of tough, durable material, and good ones will be expensive. It is better to spend the money for better gear, even if it hurts, than to risk the possiblity of stranding on some inaccessible river bank, twenty miles above the next source of help. After four or five unplanned-for days in the wilderness, with dwindling supplies, you will wish that you had paid double, triple, or more (the multiple increases in direct ratio to the amount of cold, hunger, panic and privation which you must endure) for reliable equipment and spares.

The same quality requirement holds true for the rowing frame. This must not only be made to fit your boat, but must be strongly constructed of durable materials which will be able to withstand long days of strenuous use.

You must devise some method for storing equipment so that it stays dry and protected. It is not usually suitable to drop your gear on to the fabric bottom of the boat. Impact with rocks and river debris will invariably cause damage to both the gear and the bottom; and in rapids of any sort you can expect to take water over the sides, and equipment lying in the bottom of the boat will be in for a good soaking. River running dictates a need for waterproof bags or containers, and for off-deck storage. Often this is incorporated into the rowing frame or by means of nets or lines strung along or across the hull tubes. Further, all equipment should be well secured to the boat so that in the event of overturn it is not lost downstream.

Line and spare line. It almost seems that you can never have enough line aboard a boat, and it is worth collecting and carrying a bag full to take along on all your trips. You will need line for tying up the boat, both fore and aft, for lining down tough rapids, for throwing to boats and people in trouble, for setting up camp, and for any other number of odd tying jobs. How you stow your line will be up to you, but coil it neatly and locate it so that it is immediately available when you need it.

Carry and wear personal flotation devices. It is not unusual to get tossed in the water when running rapids, and the combination of turbulence and cold can quickly tire out even a good swimmer. If you are wearing your PFD you can roll on your back, kick your feet downstream to fend off obstacles, and ride the current to safety.

First aid equipment. Make up a waterproof kit to take along on all your river trips. You should include antiseptic and sterile dressings for cuts and abrasions, Band-Aids for minor cuts and blisters, sunburn ointment, insect repellent, a snakebite kit, an elastic bandage for sprains, tweezers, aspirin, a first aid manual, and any other items which you feel might be necessary for the trip you are contemplating.

Carry a large sponge and a plastic bucket for bailing. Often, on big rapids, the boat will be half full of water by the time you reach the end.

Finally, be sure to carry your boat repair kit and pump. A failed and unrepaired chamber in a river boat can be much more of a problem than in other inflatables. The water in rapids is much more turbulent than it is in the ocean and on lakes, and the river boat is under less positive control. All-around inflation is necessary to maintain the shape of the hull, and to protect the passengers and gear from impact with obstructions in the river.

RESCUE BOATS — More and more people are turning to the water for their recreation, and communities are faced with the need for increased lifeguard and other rescue services. At the same time, personnel costs are up and municipal budgets are down. The correct solution lies in finding a less expensive but more efficient system. For larger communities the use of inflatable rescue craft can provide this.

The British were among the first to introduce inflatables into their rescue services on a large scale. The Royal National Lifeboat Institute (RNLI), which performs rescue duties of all kinds around the periphery of the British Isles, began experimenting with inflatable craft in the early 1960s. At the time their inshore rescues of swimmers, recreational boaters, etc., were increasing at an alarming rate, and the heavy, conventional, hard lifeboats which they were using were not well suited to this mission. What was required was a lighter boat with higher speed, and better handling characteristics in the surf. The inflatable proved to be the solution, and by 1963 the first ten boats were put into regular service. At this writing, there are some 152 pure inflatables, and 35 hybrids, with inflatable pontoons and fiberglass bottoms, in service

Rescue boats of the British Royal National Lifeboat Institution are supported by contributions and manned by volunteers. Their fleet of over 180 inflatables ring the British Isles and has proved to be an economic way to provide inshore rescue services for the increasing numbers of recreation minded people who find themselves in trouble at sea. (Royal National Lifeboat Institution)

Even small rescue helicopters can quickly deliver a lightweight inflatable to people in trouble in the water. (Novurania Inflatables)

around the British Isles. The program in Britain has obviously been a success, and because of this, rescue services in other parts of the world have begun to follow suit.

There are two basic ways to use an inflatable as a rescue boat. It can be kept loaded and ready on the beach or at a pier, with the crew nearby, and launched as the need arises. Alternately, it can be kept on patrol offshore, where it can instantaneously react in response to a distress call. The latter system is the most effective during the peak summer months, and is also the most efficient from the standpoint of cost effectiveness. The offshore boat can observe the beaches on its own, or react to a summons on the radio. It can replace the use of vehicles for rescues in the more remote locations, and be there faster.

For most city and county lifeguard work the optimum boat size is somewhere between 12 and 15 feet, with an engine of from 20 to 40 H.P. Boats and engines in these size ranges are large enough for equipment and personnel, small enough for easy handling on the beach and in the surf, and economical in fuel, upkeep and initial cost.

Any boat which is selected for rescue services should be able to withstand the rigors of continuous and long term hard usage. It must be made of heavy-weight fabric, reinforced at stress points, and the woodwork must be strongly constructed of top quality materials. The hull should be designed to maintain an internal pressure of no less that 2½ pounds per square inch to reduce flexing at high speeds in rough seas.

Beyond these basic requirements, most boats will need additional modifications to meet the specialized needs of the rescue services. Large, automatic self-bailers should be added, which are capable of draining a swamped boat in a minimum of time, and water-level hand holds should be mounted along the sides to provide support for persons awaiting rescue.

Rescue boats should have large, and very distinct, markings along the sides, so that they can be instantly recognized by any controlling agent on the beach and by others needing help. The engine should have a caged propeller, or a jet, and it should have a self-idling throttle in case the operator should be thrown out of the boat.

Ideally, two people should be aboard the rescue craft. This permits one to run the engine and maneuver the boat, while the other handles the rescue equipment and makes the actual pickup. Both jobs should be interchangeable as circumstances dictate.

Equipment requirements will vary depending on any number of factors. A rather extensive list of possible items of equipment is included in Appendix II for referral by interested organizations.

A well made, heavy-duty inflatable boat, equipped with a suitable engine will be far less expensive to buy, use and maintain than a four-wheel drive rescue vehicle. At the same time it can provide far greater utility and much faster response time in a rescue situation, because it delivers the rescuer to the immediate scene of the problem. As they have discovered in England, and in many other communities throughout the world, the inflatable boat is the answer to reducing the rising cost of lifeguard and other rescue services.

LIFERAFTS — While dinghies, converted for survival or otherwise, may be suitable for short-term use in an emergency, the CO-2 operated survival raft is the only piece of inflatable equipment which has been specifically designed for this service.

These vessels can truly be called rafts, since it is not their function to perform in any other capacity. The purpose of the liferaft is to remain stowed and provisioned until it is needed for survival. When this occurs, the raft is launched, in its package, a lanyard is pulled to actuate the CO-2, and it self-inflates so that survivors can climb aboard.

Good survival rafts are expensive. There are many reasons for this, but no intelligent cruising sailor can afford to be without one. Emergencies are not planned, they happen, and they must be prepared for. A good, properly equipped, self-inflating raft can ultimately mean the difference between survival or loss.

As with all things, there are both good and bad survival rafts on the market. This does not just refer to materials and workmanship. Good rafts also incorporate certain features which make survival a more assurable goal. Many of these features are costly to add, and are therefore eliminated on inexpensive substitutes.

It is worth examining some of the features which you should expect to find on any piece of quality equipment.

Naturally, good quality materials and construction are an absolute essential. Long term durability is an absolute must. The raft may be stowed on your boat, exposed to the hostile marine environment, for years before it is called into use. Even though the raft is inspected periodically, heat, moisture and chafing all take their toll. Then, if the raft is put into use, it must be able to withstand all of the abuse which continued human habitation and the sea can deliver. There are actual recorded cases where weeks, and sometimes months, have passed before rescue. It is simply not possible to expect this type of reliability and service from equipment which has been made of inferior materials, or which has been poorly constructed.

All good rafts will have a self-erecting canopy which will completely enclose the passengers and protect them from the elements. The canopy should include sealable lookout holes and vents, and an easily secured entry and exit closure. The canopy should be usable without further modification so that injured or exhausted survivors can be spared this extra effort. Rafts without protective canopies are a poor choice for long-term survival.

The raft should be chambered, but in such a way that failure of one tube will not jeopardize watertight integrity and buoyancy. This is normally accomplished by providing both an upper and a lower tube. Each tube should have sufficient buoyancy so that it, alone, can support the weight of the passengers.

Some form of stabilizing device should be added to the bottom of the raft so that it does not blow over in strong winds, or capsize when being boarded. This is usually provided in the form of a water-ballast system. That is, pockets on the bottom of the boat fill with water, which add weight.

You should look to see if hand holds are positioned around the raft, and that some type of boarding ladder is available. These can't be bulky, and are usually made of webbing which is secured to the raft by strong "D" rings or special web loops. A sea anchor should also be attached to the raft, and this should automatically deploy when the raft is actuated This will prevent the raft from skittering away before a strong wind before it can boarded, and will also keep the raft within reasonable proximity of the distress site to aid rescue efforts.

Your raft should have strongly attached towing eyes or straps included, so that the rescue vessel can tow it to safety with passengers aboard if immediate danger threatens.

Finally, some form of basic survival equipment package should be aboard. As a minimum you will want this package to include signalling equipment, a repair kit, a small bellows for topping off the raft, and possibly a sponge to use as a bailer. Note that the survival kit is often very incomplete on rafts because space for storing this extra equipment is quite limited in the packing bags and cannisters. An auxiliary survival kit, packed in a watertight container, is always recommended, and a list of suggested items which might be included is in Appendix III.

The foregoing list of desirable raft features is not exhaustive. Some rafts include many other items which can add to your comfort or assist in your rescue. Check all of the sales literature which the various manufacturers provide, and select the raft which most nearly meets the requirements for your type of cruising.

Most manufacturers offer their rafts in two different types of containers. Fiberglass canisters or boxes are provided for rafts which will be kept on deck, or otherwise subject to weathering and abuse; and fabric bags or valises are the usual choice of those which will be stowed below or in deck boxes.

Topside storage is the most desirable, since the raft is instantly available for launching in an emergency. However, topside storage does have some disadvantages. Theft becomes a greater possibility, and there is danger of loss or damage because of heavy breaking seas coming aboard.

172

Stabiliity is one important feature in survival rafts. This raft is enduring a 60-knot downdraft caused by the helicopter rotors during a U.S. Coast Guard test. (Givens Buoy Liferafts)

Rafts stowed topside need to be secured to the deck in some manner. Usually the raft is mounted on custom-made chocks, and held in place by a strap or straps made of nylon webbing or stainless steel. Quick-release buckles complete the arrangement. Many owners use a hydrostatic release which can be operated manually, or which will automatically release, because of water pressure, when they have been submerged between 5 and 15 feet below the surface. Rafts which are secured in place by a hydrostatic release should be mounted in some reasonably protected area, since they have been known to actuate under the impact of heavy crashing seas.

Locks should not be used on raft mounts for obvious reasons.

Even under the best of circumstances rafts are not designed to provide comfortable accomodations. Space is limited, and they offer little more than protection from the elements and a

173

limited amount of survival gear. Naturally, the larger the raft the more space, and while a four man raft may sound adequate for two or three people, a six or eight man will immeasurably increase whatever comfort you may be able to find as you float about. The point is, if you can afford a larger raft, buy it. The difference in price between a four, six or eight man raft is not relatively great, and neither is the weight or bulk, yet the difference in inside space is quite measurable.

Periodic inspection of survival rafts is an absolute essential. No more than a year to eighteen months should elapse between checks, and yet people tend to neglect this aspect of survival preparation. There is a tendency to believe that if a raft has received good care, inspection is a waste of money. Regretfully, it is not just the raft which needs to be inspected, but the supplies as well. How long since the batteries in the emergency light have been checked, how old is the canned water, what is the date on the flares? Have any of the metal pieces begun to corrode, and is the CO_2 unit still fully charged and connected. Most importantly, does the raft still hold air. A twenty four hour check will determine this.

The work of inspection should be done by a professional, preferably one who has been designated as a serviceman for your particular make of raft. The cost of life raft inspection in usually given as being so much per person, depending upon the rating of the raft, plus the cost of consumables which will have to be replaced. Raft inspections are rarely inexpensive, but prices do vary, and it will pay to obtain more than one estimate. Whatever you pay, the cost of an inspection is a small price if the life of your crew and yourself are at stake.

Chapter 6

Equipment and Accessories

Perhaps the majority of the people who buy inflatable boats do so because of their compactness and portability. For this reason it is important to keep non-essential equipment to a minimum. Nevertheless, there are certain items which require little space, and which can add greatly to the utility and enjoyment of your boat. Which of these you may want to choose will depend on your personal taste and requirements, of course, and on your pocketbook.

If cost is a factor, it is often possible to do your own fabricating, once you have a general idea of the design and purpose of an item. Often less expensive substitutes can be found simply by looking around in the stores in your community, and in the many discount mail-order marine catalogs. Canvas products can be fabricated at home by anyone handy with a sewing machine, or they can be made by your local awning maker. The same applies to products which lend themselves to construction out of wood.

Some accessory equipment is essential on every boat, either because the Coast Guard, or your state, says it is. Other items should be aboard because common sense and good seamanship dictate that they should. The items which fall into both of these categories will be mentioned first, with special emphasis on how they relate to or require particular consideration with inflatables.

Beyond the relatively essential items, any good inflatable store will have available a large number of other pieces of accessory equipment which may or may not be of value to you, depending on how you plan to use your boat. Choose only those accessories you need. Too much equipment in an inflatable will result in overcrowding, and complicates its use. Keep it simple, and your boating days will be much more enjoyable.

Almost any marine shop can provide you with a list of equipment which the Coast Guard deems essential or important to have aboard your boat. Foremost among these is the Personal Flotation Device, or PFD.

PFD's — The law requires that at least one PFD per person must be aboard any vessel, large or small, when operating in United States waters. In addition, every PFD must display a label which reads, "U.S. Coast Guard Approved", in order to be legal. Note that this eliminates most defacto flotation devices such as neoprene rubber wet suits, scuba diver's buoyancy compensators, and the foam rubber floats which water skiers often wear around their waists. There are four different types of PFD's available to meet the varied needs of the boating public. Types I, II, and III are all wearable devices, and Type IV is a throwable device not designed to be worn. All boats over 16 feet in length must have one Type I, II, or III device of suitable size aboard for each person, and one throwable type IV device. Boats under 16 feet in length, and that includes most inflatables, may substitute Type IV devices in place of, or in addition to, the other three types.

The most common Type IV device is the buoyant cushion, and these are an extremely good choice for an inflatable. Type IV cushions stow neatly on board, and can be used by passengers who wish to sit on the deck or the fabric floor.

176

While Type IV devices are legal to use under the circumstances outlined above, you should keep in mind that any passengers who are poor swimmers should always be required to *wear* a PFD while they are on board your boat. This is a common sense rule which should not be violated for any reason, despite the fact that the law does not make this requirement.

NAVIGATION LIGHTS — If you plan to operate your boat after dark, you must display proper navigation lights. Small rowing boats under oar or sail power alone are only required to have a white light on hand, which must be temporarily exhibited in time to prevent collision. Power boats have more complicated lighting requirements, which call for the continuous display of red and green port and starboard lights, and a white light aft.

Since most inflatables are not equipped with generators, and relatively few carry large storage batteries on board, the easiest way to comply with night lighting regulations is to purchase small "D" cell battery operated units which can be temporarily attached to the hull when needed. These are obtainable at almost all marine supply houses. Some companies, like Bonair and Zodiac, offer these small units as a part of their accessories list, and these are easy to mount and work quite well.

If you can find them, one of the better alternatives are the small battery operated units with suction cups mounted on their bases. The white light can be positioned on top of any smooth engine cowling, and the port and starboard lights, which come as one unit, usually hold well to the skin of the boat, provided that it is reasonably smooth, and that the boat is tightly inflated. If you use this type of unit, back up the suction cups by attaching a loop of line to the base in case the unit should accidentally pop off.

FIRE EXTINGUISHERS — Fire extinguishers are "not required aboard outboard motor boats less than 26 feet in length if the construction of such motorboats will not permit the entrapment of explosive or flammable gases or vapors.'' The foregoing quotation comes from a recent pamphlet (No. 290) which was issued by the Coast Guard as a guide to recreational boat owners. Realistically, almost all inflatable boats fall into this category, and the fire extinguisher is therefore not a required device. This is not to say that you should not carry one, but merely that it is not legally needed. Note, however, that if you do enclose your boat in some way, so that fumes can collect, you must add an appropriate fire extinguisher to your accessory list.

SIGNALING EQUIPMENT — What you carry in the way of signaling equipment will depend on how far you plan to stray from shore, and how much room you can spare for the storage of these items. Most boating organizations, and the Coast Guard, recommend that you carry certain basic items, like flares, smoke signals, mirrors and flashlights. This is hard to argue against, but on a space-limited inflatable it may present problems. The usual solution is to cut the list down to a few bare essentials, which can be tucked away in a spare bag, a pocket, or perhaps taped to the fuel tank.

Signaling mirrors, with aiming devices, are one easy solution. The mirror takes up almost no space, and will work, to some extent, even on rather dull days. A mirror is also persistent, and has an extremely long range, especially on a bright day. Their disadvantages are that they are limited to daytime use, and when the sun is low in the sky there is a limit to the direction in which their signal can be shown.

Orange smoke signals are a good complement to the mirror during daylight hours. The smoke is highly visible against the surrounding water, and is reasonably persistent, except on really windy days. Some are even available in combination with a flare, located on the opposite end, which can be used for signalling at night.

Naturally, if your plans call for extended cruising, or for distant trips well out into open water, then the amount of signaling equipment you carry should be increased, even at the expense of some other gear. Complete signaling kits, which contain whistles, flares, smoke, mirrors, dye markers and distress flags, are available at most chandleries. These are usually packaged in sturdy plastic boxes, which you can stow almost anywhere on board. The important thing is to realize that emergencies can happen to anyone, at any time. Your ability to signal for help may make the difference between a swift, efficient rescue, or a long, and possibly disastrous wait for help.

FIRST AID EQUIPMENT — Here is another item which is not specifically required by the Coast Guard, but which could be of vital importance in an emergency. As with distress equipment, small kits are available in both marine and drug stores. These kits contain the basic items for the initial treatment of wounds, and it is always a wise idea to carry one of these kits aboard any boat which will be operating at some distance from immediate help.

GENERAL BOATING EQUIPMENT — In addition to the foregoing, almost any boating equipment list will suggest carrying anchors, line, charts, compass and tools. For inflatables add a repair kit and an air pump. What you do in this regard is up to you. For short, nearshore trips, all of this extra equipment can probably be left at home. For longer trips you may wish to carry it all. Space may be limited, but safety must always be your primary consideration when going to sea.

The remainder of this chapter is devoted to accessories which may be of value to you, but are not required equipment. The items are listed alphabetically, for easy reference, and, in the case of unusual or hard to find items, the name of at least one major supplier will be included. The mailing address for these suppliers can be obtained by consulting the complete listing given in the appendix. Your local dealer may also be able to provide you with additional sources which are nearby and less expensive. Information on other sources will be appreciated by the publisher so that the information can be included in future editions.

BAIT TANKS — The problem of carrying live bait aboard a small boat is not exclusive to owners of inflatables. Any fisherman who plans to keep bait fish alive and active, must make some arrangement to provide a constant flow of fresh, aerated water to the storage area. On slow boats the simple solution is to tow a floating bait pen behind the boat. This works well, but for obvious reasons it becomes impractical as you increase speed. Fast fishing boats require that the bait tank be carried on board, and this means that you must employ some system for replenishing the oxygen supply, and maintaining the water in habitable condition.

For a short trip, with a small number of fish or crawdads, you can get away with an inexpensive, battery operated, aerating device. A small pump forces air through a porous stone to create a multitude of bubbles. This oxygenates the water. Unfortunately, this system does not work for longer term storage, or where a larger number of bait fish must be transported. This is not just because it will not deliver enough air, which it won't, but also because it does nothing to control temperature, which can be critical, or to maintain the correct salinity, which is important to salt water fish. To combat these problems you must use a system which circulates fresh water drawn from external sources. This requires a bit more equipment, but small units have been developed to meet this need. Aquasea, Inc., of Costa Mesa, California, is one supplier of these.

A typical bait tank assembly consists of a suitable tank, equipped with intake and outlet hoses, and a battery operated portable pump to pick up and circulate water. Tank capacities on commercial units vary, but for a space-limited inflatable you should probably restrict yourself to a unit which holds twenty gallons or less. This should be supported by a twelve volt pump capable of delivering water at the rate of about 300 gallons per hour. For a pump of this size, the smallest twelve volt automotive battery you can obtain should be a sufficient power source.

On an inflatable the transom is the only logical place to mount your water intake. Let it project slightly below the hull for optimum results. Suction cups are ideal for mounting the intake to the transom. They simplify installation, and release easily if the intake should hit something.

If you plan to make your own tank, be sure to use materials which are both non-corrosive and non-toxic. Waterproof plywood, covered with a light coat of fiberglass and resin provides the easiest solution. Construct the tank so that it is somewhat pyramidal in shape. This will reduce the free surface effect, and minimize the tendency of the water to slosh over the side when the boat is in motion. Hard plastic fittings, for connecting the hoses, can be obtained from marine dealers and stores which cater to motor home and trailer owners.

BATHING LADDERS — Some manufacturers offer these as accessory items, and they can be quite useful for boarding boats with large diameter pontoons when you are alongside in the water. If you are using swim fins, the ladder will probably be of little value. With fins most people are able to generate enough thrust to propel themselves up on to the top of the tube with a quick kick. This is not easy to do if you are using bare feet.

The ladder should be designed so that it can be draped over the side of the boat, with the upper end anchored to some solid support. The transom offers the strongest point of attachment if you bore a hole and position an eyebolt for attaching the lines. Also, be sure that your ladder extends below the boat a sufficient distance so that a swimmer can position his foot on the bottom rung comfortably. The addition of a small piece of lead to the base of the ladder will help to keep the lower rung under water. Whether you buy a ladder or make your own, make certain that the unit is light in weight, easy to stow, and constructed of materials which will not cut or chafe the hull. Ladders made of wooden rungs spliced into rope seem to work best. If your dealer does not stock ladders of this type they are easy to make, provided you use good, straight-grained wood for the rungs, and strong, rot-resistant, synthetic line.

BOAT COVERS — For inflatables which will be left permanently assembled, some sort of cover is a wise investment. The cover provides protection from the elements, and also prevents internal accumulation of water and debris. If your boat is equipped with floorboards and other wooden parts, your cover will also protect them and reduce the amount of annual maintenance required.

A good cover should be waterproof, and relatively resistant to attack by mildew or other types of fungus. It should also be made of material which is strong enough to withstand the buffeting it will receive on the highway, if trailed, or when strong winds blow.

Acrilan is the Monsanto trade name for one acrylic canvas material which is extensively used in the boating industry. This material is waterproof, comes in a variety of colors, and has an extremely long life. If you are having a custom cover made it is worth paying the extra money for fabric of this type. Your cover will look and fit better, and its longer life will more than pay for the difference in cost.

BOW DODGERS — Bow dodgers are small covers which span the bow of the boat to provide a reasonably secure and dry place for the storage of equipment. On most sportboats, ten feet in length and over, the bow dodger comes as a piece of standard equipment, already installed. This is not necessarily the case on the small sportboats, and is rarely the case with dinghies. However, most manufacturers make some provision for adding bow dodgers if these are desired.

It is difficult to say whether there is any really significant value in having a bow dodger on a soft bottomed dinghy, at least so far as providing a secure, dry storage space is concerned. They will deflect some small amount of spray, but if water is splashing against the relatively low hull tubes some will enter the boat, and anything resting on the fabric floor will be wet down, regardless. The dodger also takes up valuable space, and this is another disadvantage when they are used on dinghies.

Bow dodgers are much more useful on sportboats. Here they do serve the function for which intended, and they are necessary if a windscreen is to be mounted. They still take up space, however, and it is better if some provision is made for removing them when not needed. Some manufacturers have solved the problem by making dodgers that incorporate a zipper in the middle so that the two halves can be tied back easily, even though they remain permanently attached.

If your boat does not have a bow dodger, and has no provision for installing one, it is a relatively simple matter to fabricate your own. Use some heavy wrapping paper to make a template of your hull, and use this to cut your fabric to the proper shape. Leave about an extra inch around the periphery for a hem. Sew ties at the corners and at the centerpoints on both sides. Now cement small "D" rings to the hull at appropriate points for attaching. Alternately, you can do as the Avon people have done on some of their boats, and fasten the dodger to the hull with matching strips of the clinging "Velcro" material.

BOW STORAGE — Because high speed inflatables tend to bounce, equipment stored in the bow is prone to migrate aft. Several accessories are available which are designed to counter this movement and make this space usable.

The "forward hold-all" is a device which is offered by the Zodiac company, but which can be adapted to almost any other make of boat. The "hold-all" consists of a triangular bag, about a foot deep, which is tied to the boat by its three corners so that it is suspended about an inch above the deck. If it is covered by a bow dodger, the forward hold-all provides a reasonably dry and secure place to store lighter items like clothing, lunch bags, etc. Cameras and other light-weight fragile items can also be stored here, but they should be well padded, and housed in waterproof bags.

Bow curtains are a second alternative. The bow curtain spans the bow at the point where the tubes begin to bend inward. The base of the curtain is fixed to the thrust board, or to one of the floorboards, and the upper edge is supported at either end by hooks or ties which fasten to fittings on the hull tubes. Very often stowage pockets are sewn on to the rear face of the curtain where small items can be kept handy. The bow curtain provides an effective way to utilize the bow area for the storage of light-weight equipment.

The "forward fuel tank holder" is another offering by the Zodiac company which can be used in most other makes of inflatables. The tank holder consists of a sheet of heavy duty marine plywood, which is connected to the thrust board by fast disconnecting ring bolts. An attached strap fits over the gasoline tank to hold it in place, and small rubber chocks on the face of the plywood also help to restrict movement.

DEPTH FINDERS — These are extremely handy devices for determining bottom depth and contour, and for locating schools of fish at intermediate water levels. There are any number of portable units available which will work nicely on inflatable craft. The typical unit consists of a combination transponder/receiver, which is mounted externally on the transom, under water; and an indicating and control unit which is kept in the boat. They are powered by small lantern or flashlight batteries.

The face of the unit consists of a circular dial, coupled to a rotating arm, which causes a light to flash opposite the indicated water depth, or the echo depth of schooling fish. The sensitivity of the unit can be adjusted to eliminate or increase the intensity of minor echoes caused by weak targets at mid-water depths.

Portable depth finding units are easy to operate, and easy to maintain, but they are rarely sealed well enough to withstand the corrosive effects of salt water. If you are operating in this type of environment, the unit should be given some additional protection. The simplest solution is to enclose the indicator/control unit in one or two heavy-duty transparent plastic bags. This will permit you to see and operate the set, and still keep it safely protected from splashing water.

DOELFIN — The Doelfin is a device which is designed to assist the sportboat to make the transition to the planing position. The fin can be amazingly effective when used with boats which are heavy-laden and reluctant to drop over into a plane.

As the name implies, the device is a "V" shaped fin, which is clamped to the anti-cavitation plate of the engine with a few set screws. In cross-section the fin is shaped like an airfoil, so that when the boat is running through the water a lifting force is created at the stern. This pivots the bow downward so that the hull tubes are lying parallel to the water. In this condition drag is at a minimum, and the boat is better able to accelerate and begin planing. With heavy loads the fin often makes the difference between moving off rapidly on a plane, or plowing along slowly at displacement speeds. It is this increase in efficiency which makes the Doelfin worthwhile.

The fin is of little value if you are going to launch your boat through the surf. This is because it provides almost no lift in the aerated water, and tends to trap air beneath itself which causes the propeller to cavitate and lose effectiveness just when you need it most. To work efficiently the fin needs solid water around it. In this latter environment, when heavy loads are aboard, it is a very worthwhile piece of equipment.

DRY STORAGE — There is always some article aboard a boat which you wish to keep dry, and without special provision for this the odds in favor of dryness are not good.

Canoeists, kayakers and down-river rafters are the biggest users of waterproof containers in boating. If your dealer sells this type of craft, examine his stock of dry storage equipment. Alternatively, pick up a copy of one of the magazines which cater to the river-running public (Canoe Magazine, Downriver, Wilderness Camping), send for the many available catalogs, and order from them.

Dry storage containers come in both rigid and flexible forms. The rigid containers provide the best protection against impact damage, if that is a consideration, but they are often bulky, and require care in use to prevent chafing against the inside of your hull tubes. Dry bags are more convenient to use, and lighter, but they are also more prone to develop leaks if roughly handled. If you are relying on bags for dryness protection it is always best to double wrap your more sensitive equipment in smaller plastic bags to provide a back up layer of protection.

If you are improvising, regular household plastic bags can be used with caution. These are made of very thin material, and are not particularly durable if used without some outer covering. If you have no alternative to household bags, use several, and then surround the entire package with some sort of heavier layer, like towels or clothing. This will help to preserve the water tight integrity of the plastic, and act as a buffer against impact.

If you prefer a rigid container, and don't wish to purchase one of the commercial versions, try using covered plastic boxes, like Tupperware, and regular portable cooler chests work well to protect the more bulky items.

FLAGSTAFFS AND FLAGS — There may not be a great deal of justification for displaying a flag on a small inflatable, but everyone should be permitted to carry at least one piece of frivolous equipment on his boat, and many of us choose to fly a small American flag.

Some makes of inflatables already come with a small flagstaff mounted on the bow, in which case the problem has been solved for you. Alternately you may wish to mount a standard marine flagpole socket on top of your engine housing. Of course, all engines are different, but if your engine has a removable housing, the chances are that it will accomodate the three bolts which are necessary to mount the socket. By mounting your flagstaff in this manner, it is a simple matter to remove it at the end of the day, roll it up, and stow it with the deflated hull.

If your engine design is such that the above approach will not work, you can mount the flagstaff to the transom, using "U" bolts held in place with wing nuts for ease in disassembly. This method will require a longer staff in order to raise the flag to sufficient height to clear the engine.

FLOOR COVERINGS — A good floor covering for an inflatable should protect the woodwork against damage, and provide the occupants with a firm, easily cleaned, non-skid surface.

Carpeting, of one sort or another, is often used, but this is rarely suited to the job. All carpeting has some sort of weave to it, and after a period of time, when combined with sand and grit, this will begin to wear into the finish of the wood. Carpeting also retains moisture, mashed sandwich pieces, fish slime and bait droppings, and can become most unappetizing in a very short period of time.

One the best floor covering materials on the market is not made for the marine trade at all. This is a product called, "Anti-Fatigue Matting", which is made by the Rubbermaid company, and other manufacturers of commercial rubber products. Don't be misled by the reference to rubber. Anti-fatigue matting is made of a vinyl material that has been blown with a gas so that it is composed of countless numbers of small sealed bubbles. This is what gives it its cushioning effect when it is laid down on hard concrete decks in factories and restaurants. This is also what makes it so ideal for use in your boat. The bubbly material has been skinned over on the top with a ribbed, slightly textured, non-skid surface, and with a smooth vinyl layer on the bottom. The vinyl is relatively immune to attack by fuel and oil, and it is easily cleaned. Just as importantly, the smooth bottom is soft enough so that if gravel or shells get between it and the wooden decking, the object will push up into the matting rather than damage the paint or varnish.

Since few marine dealers stock this material, you may have to locate your own source. Check the yellow pages of your telephone book and look up suppliers under the listings for restaurant equipment, janitor supplies, industrial equipment, and other similar businesses. Failing this write to Rubbermaid, or one of the other manufacturers of rubber goods (also in the yellow pages) and ask for the name of nearby retailers.

FUEL TANKS, FLEXIBLE — These tanks are made of fabric similar to that which is used in the manufacture of your boat. Their primary value lies in their stowability when they are not full of fuel. In an empty condition fabric tanks can be tightly rolled and stored in one of the packages which contain the boat. This is particularly helpful when you must ship your equipment to another destination. The rolled tank cuts down on both the weight and bulk of the shipment, which saves both time and money.

With flexible fabric tanks most of the same precautions apply which apply to the boat. Be especially careful to avoid chafing, and certainly keep sharp objects away. The tank should always be inspected before use to insure that it still maintains its integrity against gasoline leaks. Be particularly cautious about smoking or using any type of open flame with this type of equipment on board. Even a small leak can cause an explosion.

Flexible tanks are produced by several manufacturers, and they are adaptable to any standard fuel hose.

LAUNCHING WHEELS — Helpful, and sometimes nearly essential, when launching your boat at crowded ramps, or across the beach, through the surf.

At launching ramps the primary advantage of wheels is that they permit you to completely assemble your boat next to your car, and then wheel it, full equipped, into the water. For

Launching wheels permit you to completely assemble your boat next to your car and then roll it into the water. (Lauren Hubbard)

surf launching you have the same advantage, but the primary use of wheels in surf lies in their ability to keep the engine from digging into the bottom as the inrushing water alternately raises and lowers the boat.

To be effective, wheels must have certain attributes. They must be light in weight, yet strong enough to carry the combined load of boat, motor and gear. They must be easy to maintain, and have a low susceptibility to corrosion (including wheel shaft, hubs and bearings). They must be easily stowed, and if they must be detached from the boat while at sea, either for storage or mounting, they must float.

189

Further, wheels for surf launching must be long enough to permit the engine to be completely lowered, and running, without touching the bottom.

Several companies, including Bodge and Zodiac, make excellent wheels which meet all of the above criteria, including suitability for surf work. The Load-A-Boat Company makes smaller less expensive wheels, which work well, but which are too short to allow the engine to be lowered for surf work.

In every case some form of connecting bracket must be attached to the transom of the boat. Load-A-Boat supplies this bracket with their wheels, and installation is a relatively simple matter. With the larger, surf capable, wheels the mounting bracket is often sold as an additional accessory, and this cost, and often the cost of mounting, must be added to the overall price. (Note that some boat manufacturers install mounting brackets, which are compatible with their own wheels, on their boats as standard equipment.)

SAILING EQUIPMENT — Sailing equipment for inflatables is not inexpensive, but then it is not inexpensive for hard boats either. The material which goes into sails and related equipment is going to cost money because it must be strong and resistant to marine corrosion. Labor is also costly, because sails must be cut to exacting shapes to draw effectively.

With regard to efficiency, probably the most important consideration is how the mast is guyed. The mast must remain perpendicular to the hull, and supporting cables which run directly to the hull pontoons are rarely very efficient. This is because there is a certain amount of flexing and give in all inflatables, even when they are tightly inflated. If the stays are attached directly to some portion of the fabric hull, the boat will bend as soon as pressure is applied to the sail. As the boat bends the stays will slacken and the mast will no longer remain vertical.

In an inflatable, the only really effective system for maintaining the mast in the correct position is to anchor it to some solid structural member which is independent of the hull. The best way to achieve this is to bridge the hull with a securely fastened frame of wood or metal. This frame can then be used to anchor the mast in the center, and supporting stays can be run down and connected on either side. The boat can then flex and twist, but the tension on the mast will still remain constant. This is the system which most inflatable sailing craft employ today.

The frame can also be used to mount the leeboards, which are necessary to keep the boat from sliding sideways in the water.

Many of the sailing kits put out by inflatable boat manufacturers are adaptable to use on other makes of boats, usually by the simple addition of a few fittings. Naturally, this works best when the boat of intended use is similar in size and configuration to the one for which the sail was originally intended.

SCUBA TANK RACKS — If you have ever had to put up with loose scuba tanks rolling around in the bottom of a boat, you will appreciate the fine metal tank racks being produced by a company called Pelican Products, in Torrance, California. These racks, which look like enlarged versions of the old fashioned milk bottle containers, hold your tanks in an upright position and give you much better utilization of your existing space. Pelican makes them to hold either four or six bottles, and supplies the racks with rubber bumpers around the rim to keep the tanks from rattling. The heavy metal wire, which forms the rack, has been dipped in plastic to seal it and prevent rust. Pelican suggests that for maximum stability you add a plywood base, extending six inches beyond the sides. From experience this is not absolutely necessary, since the weight of the metal bottles tends to anchor the rack nicely.

If you should choose to make your own rack, make it good and sturdy. The continuous jolting by the heavy bottles, as they rock back and forth with the movement of the boat, will rapidly destroy any rack which is weakly made.

SEATING — Since many makes of inflatables do not come with seats, the inflatable owner is often left to his own devices to provide these. As we mentioned in Chapter 5, sitting on the hull pontoons is one acceptable solution, so long as the water is smooth, radical maneuvers are avoided, and hand holds are available and used. However, on those occasions when the hull pontoons will not serve, the occupants of the boat must be given other alternatives.

Inflatable seats are one solution. These come in several configurations, the three most common being the cylindrical "thwart" seat, the single inflated "pillow" seat, and the same "pillow" seat with an inflated back rest.

The "thwart" seat is most often used in dinghies, although there are some exceptions to this in the smaller sport boats. The seat consists of an air-filled fabric cylinder, about the same diameter as the hull tubes, which spans the boat forming a round thwart for sitting. Usually "D" rings, or other attaching devices, are cemented to the ends or sides, to secure the seat in the desired location. The seat will also have a filler valve located somewhere on the side. Thwart seats are handy because they can be moved about, they stow easily, and they provide extra flotation. They must fit tightly, or be well secured, or they will roll, and they tend to be expensive because of the costs of the fabric, attaching devices, filler valve, and labor.

The inflated "pillow" seats, both with and without backs, are reminiscent of small air mattresses. The seat and back portions are ribbed to provide a series of parallel tubes. The seat sits on the deck, where it provides between six and eight inches of insulation between your behind and the bottom of the boat. If the seat is one of those with a back, some type of strap will be provided, which is anchored on either side of the boat to provide support. As with the "thwart" seat, it is usual to have some provision for tying the seat base in the desired location. "Pillow" seats are commonly used in sportboats where they keep the occupants seated well down inside the hull for protection and security. "Pillow" seats have the same advantages as "thwart" seats, but fit is not so critical. They may, or may not, be expensive, depending on the materials used in construction. Many are made of heavy, unreinforced vinyl, which is relatively inexpensive and easily machine fabricated. These seem to work satisfactorily, and should not be too expensive.

"Pillow" seats are bouncy, and if you are seated on one in the forward part of the boat when she is running over choppy seas, you can expect to spend part of your time airborne. Poor space utilization is also a problem because the low-lying seat positions you so that your legs are stretched out along the deck of the boat.

Another regularly used type of seating is the so-called "board" seat. As the name implies, this is nothing more than a good strong board, which spans the boat, with the ends resting on pontoons. The board ends are beveled slightly to conform to the shape of the hull, and are covered with fabric to minimize chafing. Lines are attached, which can be tied in a variety of ways to prevent the board from moving. Because chafing is inevitable, even with padded ends, if the boat is used frequently, it is a good idea to add a second layer of hull material to the pontoon tops in the area where the board will rest.

One of the advantages of the board seat is that it raises the passengers up off the deck into a more comfortable sitting position. This also permits better utilization of interior space, since it allows other equipment to be stowed below the passengers on the deck.

If you plan to fabricate a board seat of your own design, be certain to select a strong, straight grained piece of wood, at least an inch to an inch-and-a-quarter in thickness. This will depend on the distance the board must span. The strain on the board can be tremendous when the boat is running at high speed over the waves. Thin, brittle wood, or wood with large knot holes or imperfections, will not be able to stand up under the heavy pounding.

In a boat the gasoline tank is always a problem. It takes up valuable space, and it is invariably coated with a thin coating of oil and imbedded dirt. The simple solution is to store the tank in a box, which can also serve as a seat. In this way you kill two birds with one stone. The tank is covered, and the space can be used for seating. The Zodiac company carries these on their accessory list, and their boxes are very well made of mahogany marine plywood. They are also very expensive. A much less costly alternative, made of fiberglass, can be obtained from Ocean Ventures in San Diego, California. Both the Ocean Ventures and Zodiac box seats are designed to hold a standard six gallon gasoline tank, and have some additional room at one end for miscellaneous items like first aid kits, flares, tools, or even one or two local charts. Since some spillage from the tank is inevitable, anything which will be adversely effected by gasoline or oil should be well wrapped, or stowed elsewhere.

If you plan to make a box seat of your own, it is important that the sides be smooth to prevent chafing, and that a series of drain holes be cut in the bottom to give spilled fuel an exit. For hand grips, cut some properly shaped holes in either end, which serve the additional purpose of venting gasoline fumes.

For the fisherman who desires a seat with a swiveling base, these are available through most marine dealers. The Garelick Manufacturing Company, in Minnesota, is one of the larger manufacturers of this type equipment for small boats. Their catalog, which any dealer can obtain, contains a large number of swivel seat alternatives, including small units which can be clamped or bolted to board seats or fuel tank seat boxes. Also available is a molded fiberglass seat, which swivels on its own square fiberglass base. The base has one side cut open to allow storage beneath.

As mentioned in Chapter 5, imagination counts when inflatable boat seating arrangements are being considered. Different circumstances require different solutions, and efficient space utilization should always be one of the paramount goals.

SELF-BAILERS — If your sportboat is not already equipped with self-bailing ports, you might find it worthwhile to install them. Self-bailers in their simplest form are nothing more than holes in the transom which permit internal water to escape when the boat is moving. Since this action stops when the boat stops, it is also necessary to have a plug available, or some form of one way stopper device, to keep the water from flowing back into the boat when power is reduced.

Almost any marine store can provide you with self-bailers, and with a little care and a few tools it is a simple matter to install them yourself. Self-bailers work best if installed near the centerline of the boat, and below the floorboards. This usually places them fairly close to the base of the transom, so care must be taken when drilling the hole. Use a spade bit of the proper diameter on an electric drill, if you have one. If you have never used a bit of this type, make a test run on some scrap wood before working on your boat. It is important to keep the drill bit perpendicular to the surface to avoid slicing into the bottom fabric. The floorboards should be removed from the boat in order to give yourself a clear area in which to work.

When you go shopping for self-bailers, insist on the type which incorporate a one-way flow device. This saves you the trouble of reaching down and installing a stopper plug each time you reduce power. Even if your one-way device leaks a bit, or should fail completely, you have very little to worry about. The boat will merely settle until the pontoon buoyancy takes over, and then the inward flow of water will stop.

If your boat is already equipped with a self-bailer, but one which does not incorporate a one-way device, there are attachments which can provide this feature.

One of these, made by DePersia in Grand Haven, Michigan, consists of a smooth plastic housing which is screwed onto the transom over the bailer port. The housing contains a ball which drops in place, covering the hole, when the boat slows or comes to a stop. This ball is pushed aside when forward motion is resumed and water is seeking to escape.

Another of the one-way flow controls is manufactured by Tempo Products Company, in Cleveland, Ohio. This small device consists of a rubber insert which is placed in the existing hole, and which has an outer end which is flattened out so that the two sides contact each other. The flattened portion can expand outward to permit internal water to exit, but when the pressure outside is greater the two sides are pressed together and inward water flow is restricted.

Both of these devices are inexpensive, and equally satisfactory. They can be permanently installed without any effect on the boat or its stowability.

SUN CANOPIES — If you operate in an area where intense sun is a problem, it is a surprisingly simple matter to mount a standard hard-boat folding sun canopy on most inflatable sportboats. What is required is some sort of wooden footing that will permit the attachment of the hardware to support the canopy frame. If your sportboat has a raised anti-hogging strip along the top of the tubes, this is the best place to anchor your footing pieces. Bolt a block of wood to the strip on each side, padding the base with fabric

Sun canopies can be rigged on most inflatables just as they can on hard boats.
(Ocean Ventures, San Diego, CA)

so that it does not chafe into the hull tubes. Back your bolts with large washers, or with another smaller strip of wood, so that they do not tear through the material when under strain.

If you do not have an anti-hogging strip, you may be able to use your oarlock mounts; and if these are not satisfactory, cement blocks of wood in place using hull material and repair cement. You should be able to obtain both of these from your inflatable dealer.

Once the swivelling base of your canopy is anchored to the wood blocks, it can be raised to the vertical position and tensioning straps at the four corners can be fastened to the hull of the boat. Use any existing grommet holes or "D" rings to secure them. If you lack these, cement on your own as necessary. You can also use the bow eye and transom as connecting points if you have tensioning straps of sufficient length.

Keep the tensioning straps tight so as to minimize canopy movement as the boat bucks along over the water surface. Excessive motion can cause fatigue in the attaching fittings, so it is wise to inspect these periodically for wear.

WINDSCREENS — Most inflatable boat manufacturers make some provision for attaching a windscreen to their sportboat models. The primary advantage of the windscreen is that it affords the passengers in the boat some protection from the wind and spray. They are especially helpful, and often necessary, when you are running in cold climates in bad weather. However, windscreens also have some disadvantages. Generally they are a problem to store and carry because of their size and vulnerability to scratching. Additionally, many of them have a dangerously sharp, exposed upper edge, which will cut or abrade passengers very readily if they should accidentally fall against it. Covering the edge with two or three layers of strong plastic tape will eliminate the latter problem.

It is fairly standard procedure to attach the windscreen to the boat along the after edge of the bow dodger, and this, in turn, must be supported in some way so that the screen is high enough to do its job. The bow dodger support, then, is one additional piece of equipment which must be carried.

If you are thinking about buying a windscreen for your boat, examine the unit for its relative ease of installation and storage. If these are not present then it is doubtful that the screen will see much use after the first or second try. The thickness of the plastic material should also be checked, since material which is too thin will buckle in the wind, and plastic which is too thick will not be supple enough to bend with the boat.

The number of accessory items which are available to small craft owners is almost infinite, and it is one function of any salesperson to make you want to buy as many of these extras as possible. The percentage profit margin on smaller pieces of equipment is greater than on the basic boat, and the total dollar profit can often be nearly doubled by accessory sales. Every inflatable boat needs some additional equipment. Very few need very much. Forewarned is forearmed. Buy your boat, PFD's, an anchor and some line, try it out, and *then* decide what extra equipment you will need. If you keep it simple you'll keep it sailing.

Chapter 7

Inflatable Boat Manufacturers & Importers

One of the most satisfying developments in the inflatable boat business has been the rapid growth in the number of manufacturers and importers now offering their products in the United States. This has opened up some entirely new buying opportunities for the American public so that they are now able to obtain inflatables of virtually any size or type to meet their boating needs. Colored boats are beginning to be offered and accepted in far greater numbers than ever before, and this trend appears to be accelerating. Design innovations are being introduced with greater frequency by many manufacturers in order to appeal to American preferences. While all this is quite healthy for the inflatable boat industry, it has imposed a burden on the consumer who wishes to be aware of all of the options available. The information in this chapter has been included to assist in this regard.

The following alphabetical listing is intended to be a guide to the various types and kinds of inflatable boats currently available in the United States. The material has been compiled by using catalogs, and by personal contact with the companies involved. Because of space limitations, and for consistency (since not all companies provide the same information or provide it in the same form), the data is given in condensed form and confines itself to major points of comparison. For additional current information the reader should contact the company concerned and request a copy of the latest catalog. Manufacturers and importers are invited and encouraged to forward corrections or updated material to the publisher for inclusion in future editions of this book.

PART I: DINGHIES, KAYAKS AND CANOES, SPORTBOATS, RIVERBOATS AND HYBRID CRAFT

ACHILLES (Japan)

ACHILLES INFLATABLE CRAFT
25 Branca Road,
East Rutherford, NJ 07073
(201) 438-6400

FABRIC TYPE: Nylon coated with a neoprene/Hypalon mixture.
DINGHIES: Standard equipment — Bow ring, painter, towing rings (ST-5 only), detachable bow dodger, rubbing strake, lifelines, outboard bracket, oars, oar retainers, two seats, wooden floorboards, lifting handles (ST-4 and 5 and DT-4 only), pump, carrying bag, repair kit. Color: Grey.

ACHILLES dinghies come in two models: Deluxe models (designated DT) have two wooden seats. Super-Deluxe models (designated ST) have a wooden seat aft and an inflated thwart seat forward.

MODEL	LENGTH	BEAM	TUBE (DIA.)	WT. (LBS.)	CAP. (LBS.)	MAX. ENG H.P.
DT-2/ST-2	8'4"	4'1"	11.8"	48	550	4
DT-4/ST-4	9'5"	4'7"	13.8"	64	792	4
ST-5	10'4"	4'9"	13.8"	68	1188	4

SPORT DINGHIES (Sportboats capable of operation with or without floorboards). Standard equipment — Bow ring, painter, detachable bow dodger, rubbing strake, lifelines, oars, oar retainers, a wooden and inflated thwart seat, pump, carrying bag, repair kit. Color: Grey.

MODEL	LENGTH	BEAM	TUBE (DIA.)	WT. (LBS.)	CAP. (LBS.)	MAX. ENG H.P.
SPD-2	9'2"	4'1"	11.8"	40	550	6/5 *
SPD-4	10'2"	4'7"	13.8"	51	792	7.5/6 *

*With/without floorboards.

SPORTBOATS: Standard equipment — Inflatable keel, marine plywood floorboards, bow ring, painter, bow dodger (fixed on SR series, detachable on SD series), rubbing strake, lifelines, oarlocks (except SR-44 and 52), fitting points for seats, windscreen (SR series only), self-bailers, lifting handles, anti-splash vanes, pump, carrying bag, repair kit. Color: Grey.

MODEL	LENGTH	BEAM	TUBE	WT.	CAP.	MAX. H.P.
SD-11	10'8"	4'7"	14'8"	90	880	20
SD-12	12'0"	5'1"	15.8"	101	1100	25
SD-13	13'2"	5'7"	17.7"	156	1320	35
SR-108	10'8"	4'7"	14.8"	95	880	20
SR-124	12'4"	5'1"	15.8"	117	1100	25
SR-132	13'2"	5'7"	17.7"	161	1320	35
SR-140	14'0"	5'7"	17.7"	167	1540	35
SR-44	14'3"	6'1"	19.7"	216	1760	45
SR-52	16'9"	6'11"	21.6"	264	1980	50**

**Long shaft engine

AVON INFLATABLES LIMITED (England)

North and Southeastern States:
IMTRA CORPORATION
151 Mystic Avenue,
Medford, MA 02155
(617) 391-5660

Midwest and Central Eastern States:
INLAND MARINE COMPANY
79 East Jackson Street,
Wilkes-Barre, PA 18701
(717) 822-7185

Western States, Texas, Alaska:
SEAGULL MARINE
1851 McGaw Avenue,
Irvine, CA 92714
(714) 979-6161

Canada:
AVON INFLATABLES OF CANADA LIMITED
1410 Spears Road,
Oakville, Ontario L6L 5M
(416) 827-6919

FABRIC TYPE: Nylon coated with a neoprene/Hypalon mixture.
DINGHIES: Standard equipment — Bow ring, painter, bow dodger cleats, rubbing strake, lifelines, fittings for outboard bracket, molded oarlocks, inflatable thwart seat(s), fiberglass stern seat (Redcrest and Redseal only), pump, carrying bag, repair kit. Color: Grey.

MODEL	LENGTH	BEAM	TUBE (DIA.)	WT. (LBS.)	CAP. (LBS.)	MAX. ENG H.P.
Redstart	8'2"	4'0"	12"	36	550	3
Redcrest	9'3"	4'6"	13"	43	700	4
Redseal	10'3"	4'10"	14"	51	950	4
Redshank	12'3"	5'6"	15"	62	1250	6

SPORTBOATS: Standard equipment — Inflatable keel, marine plywood floorboards, bow handle, painter, bow dodger and bow dodger cleats (depends on model), rubbing strake, lifelines, oarlocks (except S-550 and S-650), fiberglass seat (Sport tender 10 and S-300 only), self-bailers, pump, carrying bag, repair kit. The following items are included on all boats except the S-60 and Sport tender 10: ski hooks, lifting handles, pressure gauge, anti-splash vanes. Color: Grey.

MODEL	LENGTH	BEAM	TUBE (DIA.)	WT. (LBS.)	CAP. (LBS.)	MAX. ENG H.P.
S-60 Sport dinghy	9'0"	4'4"	14/13"*	69/47**	600	8/6**
Sport tender 10	10'0"	4'10"	14.5"	90	800	10
S-250	10'6"	4'10"	15/13.5"*	111	800	25
S-300	12'9"	5'6"	17"	142	1250	30
S-400	12'9"	5'6"	17"	144	1250	45
S-550	14'6"	6'2"	19/16.5"*	219	1800	55
S-650	16'6"	6'10"	21/18"*	262	2500	65

*Largest/smallest diameter of tapered hull tubes.
**With/without floorboards.

202

HYBRID BOATS: Searider series — Standard equipment — Rigid "V" shaped fiberglass lower hull, bowhandle and painter, bow dodger, rubbing strake, lifelines, upholstered seats, windscreen, self-bailers, lifting handles, ski hooks, remote steering, steering console, fuel tank fittings, pressure gauge, pump, repair kit. Color: Grey.

MODEL	LENGTH	BEAM	TUBE (DIA.)	WT. (LBS.)	CAP. (LBS.)	MAX. ENG H.P.
SR4M	13'4"	5'11"	17/15"*	283	1100	50
SR5M	17'11"	6'8"	18.5/ 16.5"*	630	1650	120

*Largest/smallest diameter of tapered hull tubes.

RIVERBOATS: Standard equipment — Bow and stern handles, 16 heavy duty "D" rings, rubbing strakes, lifting handles, two storage pockets, recessed valves, pump, repair kit. Color: Grey.

Adventurer	13'9"	6'8"	18"	99	2100
Professional	15'9"	7'4"	20"	114	2750
Spirit	18'0"	8'0"	21"	154	3600

BARAKUDA (Germany)

ELCO MARINE SALES
21912 Winnebago Street,
El Toro, CA 92630
(714) 581-3111

FABRIC TYPE: Polyester coated with ethylavenvinylacetate.

DINGHIES: Standard equipment — Bow ring, lifelines, fittings for outboard bracket, oarlocks, wooden seats, floorboards, pump, carrying bag, repair kit. Color: International orange.

SB-20	6'7"	3'9"	12"	37	440	3
SB-22	7'3"	3'9"	12"	42	550	3
SB-25	8'2"	3'11"	12"	46	770	3

SPORTBOATS: Standard equipment — Inflatable keel, marine plywood floorboards, bow ring, towing connectors, rubbing strake, lifelines, pump, carrying bag, repair kit. Elbe series boats have the following additional equipment: Bow dodger, lifting handles, windscreen, self-bailers.

BARAKUDA sportboats come in two models:
Weser models are lighter weight stripped down boats.

Elbe models are heavier, take heavier engines, and include the additional equipment listed above.

MODEL	LENGTH	BEAM	TUBE (DIA.)	WT. (LBS.)	CAP. (LBS.)	MAX. ENG H.P.
Weser III	9'10"	4'9"	14/12"*	66	880	10
Weser II	11'6"	5'3"	16/14"*	100	1345	15
Elbe III	9'10"	4'7"	14/12"*	119	880	40
Elbe II	11'10"	5'3"	16/14"*	143	1350	45
Elbe I	13'2"	5'11"	18/16"*	178	2000	55

*Largest/smallest diameter of tapered hull tubes.

BOMBARD (France)

J.P. HUGHES INTERNATIONAL, INC.
523 West 6th Street, Suite 361
Los Angeles, CA 90014
(213) 626-5710

FABRIC TYPE: Polyester coated with a neoprene/Hypalon mixture.
DINGHIES: Standard equipment — Lifelines, oarlocks, slatted wooden floor inserts, carrying bag, repair kit, hand bellows. Color: Orange.

The AX-1 and AX-2 are conventionally shaped dinghies with a continuous, all-around, compartmented hull tube.

The AX-3 is a "U" shaped sport-tender.

AX-1	6'11"	3'9"	13"	25	800	
AX-2	8'8"	4'1"	13"	33	1100	4
AX-3	9'4"	4'8"	14"	49	1212	6

SPORTBOATS: Standard equipment — Wooden keel, marine plywood floorboards, bow handle, painter, bow dodger, windscreen, rubbing strakes, lifelines, oarlocks, self-bailers, (except Bombard 1 Super), lifting handles, foot bellows, carrying bags, repair kit, Ski-Tow rings (except Bombard 1 Super, 2 & 2S, Commando 6), Pressure gauge (except 1 Super, 2 & 2S, 3 & 3S), oars or paddles (except 1 Super, 2 & 2S). Color: Grey or blue (Bombard models); Black (Commando models).

BOMBARD sportboats come in two models:
"Bombard" models are the standard boats in the line.
"Commando" models are built of heavier weight fabric.

Bombard 1 Super	9'4"	4'8"	14"	70	1212	10
Bombard 2 & 2S	10'4"	4'8"	15"	99/105	1480	20
Bombard 3	11'10"	5'1"	16"	132	1874	25

MODEL	LENGTH	BEAM	TUBE (DIA.)	WT. (LBS.)	CAP. (LBS.)	MAX. ENG H.P.
Bombard 3S	12'6"	5'7"	18"	177	2333	40
Bombard 4	14'5"	5'7"	18"	209	2655	50
Bombard 5	15'5"	6'7"	20"	248	3638	65
Commando 3	11'10"	5'1"	16"	132	1874	25
Commando 4	14'5"	5'7"	18"	209	2655	50
Commando 5	15'5"	6'7"	20"	248	3638	65
Commando 6	19'8"	7'10"	22"	418	4410	115

BONAIR BOATS (USA)

BONAIR BOATS
15501 W. 109th Street,
Lenexa, KS 66219
(913) 888-8484

FABRIC TYPE: Nylon coated with PVC.

DINGHY: Standard equipment — Bow ring, detachable seat, oars, pump, carrying bag, repair kit. Color: White.

D-300	9'10"	5'4"	15.5"	45	900	5

SPORTBOATS: Standard equipment — Inflatable keel, marine plywood floorboard, bow handles, bow dodger, rubbing strake, lifelines, oarlocks, fittings for seats, self-bailers (Brute models only), lifting handles, pump, carrying bag, repair kit. Color: Bonair models — white or grey; Brute models — grey.

BONAIR sportboats come in two models:
Bonair models are the standard boats in the line.
Brute models are built of heavy weight fabric for commercial as well as recreational use.

Bonair I	11'8"	5'4"	15.5"	95	900	25
Bonair II	13'0"	5'8"	15.5"	115	1000	35
Bonair III	14'8"	6'2"	15.5"	140	1130	40
Brute 400	13'0"	5'8"	15.5"	125	1000	45
Brute 500	16'5"	6'5"	17.5"	170	2500	60

SPECIALTY CRAFT: SEA SLED — The "Sled" consists of a single 22″ inflated tube supported by two 12″ outrigger tubes. It is designed to be ridden upon and towed by another vessel.

MODEL	LENGTH	BEAM	TUBE (DIA.)	WT. (LBS.)	CAP. (LBS.)	MAX. ENG H.P.
Sea Sled	16′6″	3′6″	22/12″	40	3000	

BOSTON WHALER (France)

BOSTON WHALER INC.
1149 Hingham Street,
Rockland, MA 02370
(617) 871-1400

FABRIC TYPE: Nylon coated with PVC.

DINGHY: Standard equipment — Bow ring, towing rings, rubbing strake, lifelines, fittings for outboard bracket, oarlocks, oars, pump, repair kit. Color: Off white.

MODEL	LENGTH	BEAM	TUBE (DIA.)	WT. (LBS.)	CAP. (LBS.)	MAX. ENG H.P.
Tender BW270D	9′0″	4′9″	16.5″	46	1075	4*

*Long shaft engine.

SPORTBOATS: Standard equipment — Inflatable keel, marine plywood floorboards, bow rings, towing rings, bow dodger, rubbing strake, lifelines, oars, oar retainers, wooden seat, self-bailers, pump, repair kit. Color: Off white.

MODEL	LENGTH	BEAM	TUBE (DIA.)	WT. (LBS.)	CAP. (LBS.)	MAX. ENG H.P.
BW270S	9′0″	4′9″	16.5″	55	827	6
BW310S	10′2″	4′8″	16.5″	95	1052	10
BW340S	11′3″	5′6″	17.7″	103	1311	15

CALLEGARI (Italy)

BRITISH MOTOR CAR DISTRIBUTORS, LTD.
19100 Susana Road
Compton, CA 90221
(213) 774-9831

FABRIC TYPE: Polyester coated with neoprene/Hypalon mixture.

DINGHY: Standard equipment — Towing and lifting shackles, lifelines, outboard bracket, oars, oar retainers, inflatable thwart seat, pump, carrying bag, repair kit. Color: Orange.

MODEL	LENGTH	BEAM	TUBE (DIA.)	WT. (LBS.)	CAP. (LBS.)	MAX. ENG H.P.
Rev Mare 2000/1	8′4″	4′6″	12″	29	625	4

SPORTBOATS: Standard equipment — Wooden keel (Airone has an inflatable keel), marine plywood floorboards, bow ring or handle, bow dodger (except Jumbo models), rubbing strake, lifelines, oars or paddles and retainers, self-bailers, lifting handles (most models), pump, carrying bag, repair kit. Color: Varies with model (see below).

CALLEGARI sportboats come in four different models:

Jumbo models — rectangular shape, no bow dodger. Color: Yellow.

Airone Model — Has inflatable keel, lace-on overall cover. Color: Yellow.

America models — Have a fixed bow dodger, bow curtain with waterproof pocket, seats as standard equipment. Color: Orange.

Professional models — Have detachable bow dodgers, include two of the largest boats imported into the USA. Color: Grey.

MODEL	LENGTH	BEAM	TUBE (DIA.)	WT. (LBS.)	CAP. (LBS.)	MAX. ENG H.P.
Jumbo Models						
Jumbo	11'6"	5'4"	15.5"	143	950	20
Super-Jumbo	13'3"	5'9"	17"	165	1250	30
Airone Model						
Airone	12'8"	5'0"	16"	96	950	15
America Models						
Condor America	10'2"	4'6"	15.3"	84	950	12
Alcione America	11'4"	5'3"	17.3"	114	1000	28
Super-Alcione Am.	13'2"	5'9"	18.5"	145	1330	40
Professional Models						
Alcione	11'4"	5'3"	17.3"	110	1000	28
Nibbio	13'9"	5'10"	18.5"	171	1550	50
Albatross	15'11"	7'1"	22.7"	273	2500	65
Super-Albatross	20'0"	8'1"	23.5"	451	3500	120
Oceanic	27'11"	11'3"	31.5"	990	5500	250

CAMPWAYS (Japan and USA)

CAMPWAYS
12915 S. Spring Street,
Los Angeles, CA 90061
(213) 532-0910

FABRIC TYPE: Nylon coated with neoprene/Hypalon mixture (Sea Scamp and Sea Rider dinghies of nylon coated with neoprene).

DINGHIES: Standard equipment — Bow ring, rubbing strake, lifelines, fittings for outboard bracket, molded oarlocks, repair kit. Cormorant models also include: detachable bow dodger, wooden and inflatable seats, carrying bag and pump. Color: Cormorants and Sea Scamp — Grey; Sea Riders — Blue.

MODEL	LENGTH	BEAM	TUBE (DIA.)	WT. (LBS.)	CAP. (LBS.)	MAX. ENG H.P.
Cormorant 8'	8'0"	4'0"	11.5"	37	575	3
Cormorant 9'8"	9'8"	4'6"	13"	55	850	4
Sea Scamp	10'0"	4'8"	14"	32	1060	3
Sea Rider 10'	10'0"	5'0"	14"	50	1195	4
Sea Rider 12"	12'0"	5'8"	16"	59	1600	4

SPORTBOATS: Standard equipment — Inflatable keel, aluminum floorboards (Sea Wind has wooden boards), bow handle, bow dodger, rubbing strake, lifelines, molded oarlocks, lifting handles, repair kit. The Sea Wind does *not* have the following items which are standard on the other sportboats: Self-bailers, painter, pump, carrying bags. Color: Grey.

MODEL	LENGTH	BEAM	TUBE (DIA.)	WT. (LBS.)	CAP. (LBS.)	MAX. ENG H.P.
Sea Wind 12'	12'0"	4'8"	16"	88	1500	15
Argonaut 12'4"	12'4"	5'3"	16.5"	156	1700	35
Argonaut 13'6"	13'6"	5'8"	19.5"	190	2100	40
Argonaut 15'0"	15'0"	5'9"	21"	215	2800	55

RIVERBOATS: Standard equipment — Heavy duty "D" rings, recessed valves, rubbing strake, inflatable thwart seats, lifelines, motor mount bracket, repair kit. Color: Grey.

MODEL	LENGTH	BEAM	TUBE (DIA.)	WT. (LBS.)	CAP. (LBS.)	MAX. ENG H.P.
Sea Rider 14'	14'0"	6'8"	19"	70	2700	5
Nantahala	11'0"	5'5"	15"	88	1400	5
Chattooga	13'0"	6'0"	18"	113	2340	6
Piute	11'0"	5'5"	15"	52	1470	6
Hopi	12'0"	6'0"	17"	66	1800	5

MODEL	LENGTH	BEAM	TUBE (DIA.)	WT. (LBS.)	CAP. (LBS.)	MAX. ENG H.P.
Apache 12 '	12 '0 "	6 '0 "	16 "	98	2000	8
Apache 15 '	15 '0 "	6 '6 "	18 "	141	3400	10
Miwok II	13 '6 "	6 '7 "	19 "	130	2660	7
Shoshoni	16 '0 "	6 '9 "	19 "	154	3000	8
Shoshoni Mk. V	17 '6 "	7 '8 "	21 "	197	4200	8
Havasu	18 '0 "	7 '8 "	21 "	203	4300	8

*Note that the Sea Rider 10 ' and 12 ' are also adaptable for river running.

DYER BOATS

DYER BOAT COMPANY — THE ANCHORAGE
67 Miller Street,
Warren, RI 02885
(401) 245-3301

FABRIC TYPE: Nylon coated with neoprene/Hypalon.

DINGHY: Standard equipment — Bow ring, rubbing strake, lifelines, bow dodger, wooden and inflatable seats, molded oarlocks, carrying bag, pump, repair kit. Color: Grey.

Duck	9 '8 "	4 '6 "	13 "	55	715	4

EXPLORER BOATS (USA)

EXPLORER BOAT COMPANY
145 Industrial Parkway,
P.O. Box 108,
Ithaca, MI 48847
(517) 875-2025

FABRIC TYPE: Polyester coated with PVC.

DINGHY: Standard equipment — Bow handle, bow dodger with zipper, rubbing strake, lifelines, fittings for outboard brackets, oarlocks, fittings for seat, pump, carrying bag, repair kit. Color: Light blue.

Dinghy	9 '0 "	4 '7 "	15 "	45	700	4

SPORTBOATS: Standard equipment — Inflatable keel, marine plywood floorboards, bow handle, painter, bow dodger with zipper, rubbing strake, lifelines, oarlocks, fittings for seat(s), pump, carrying bag, repair kit. Color: Light blue.

MODEL	LENGTH	BEAM	TUBE (DIA.)	WT. (LBS.)	CAP. (LBS.)	MAX. ENG H.P.
Discovery I	9'10"	4'10"	15"	90	800	15
Discovery II	10'6"	4'10"	15"	95	900	20
Discovery III	12'6"	5'6"	17"	130	1200	30
Discovery IV	14'6"	6'2"	17"	170	1900	35

HUTCHINSON (France)

PORT CITY MARINE COMPANY
1212 South 13th Street,
P.O. Box 3767,
Wilmington, NC 28406
(919) 343-1789

FABRIC TYPE: Nylon coated with neoprene/Hypalon mixture.

DINGHIES: Standard equipment — Bow ring, painter, rubbing strake, lifelines, fittings for outboard bracket, oarlocks, inflatable pillow seat (except the "82" boats) slatted floorboards, pump, carrying bag, repair kit. Color: Orange.

Dinghy 220	7'3"	4'0"	12"	33	584	2
Dinghy 260	8'7"	4'5"	13"	46	783	4
Dinghy 290	9'6"	4'8"	14"	51	970	4
N-82 Sport Dinghy	9'4"	4'6"	14"	44	937	4
Mapa 82 Sport Dinghy	9'4"	4'6"	14"	46	937	4

CANOE: Standard equipment — Carrying bag, pump, repair kit. Color: Orange.

Marsouin	10'10"	3'0"	10"	24	441	*

*Sailing equipment available as an optional extra.

SPORTBOATS: Standard equipment — Wooden keel, marine plywood floorboards, bow handle, bow dodger (except N-102), rubbing strake, lifelines, oarlocks, oar retainers, windscreen (except N-102), self-bailers (252 boats and larger), pump, carrying bag, repair kit. Color: Mapa series - Orange; N series - Blue grey.

HUTCHINSON sportboats come in two models:

Mapa series are constructed of slightly heavier material and have an anti-hogging strip on top of the hull tubes.

N series are a lighter weight stripped down version of the Mapa boats.

MODEL	LENGTH	BEAM	TUBE (DIA.)	WT. (LBS.)	CAP. (LBS.)	MAX. ENG H.P.
Mapa 102	9'10"	4'5"	14"	64	926	7.5
Mapa 202	11'0"	4'9"	15"	112	1125	20*
Mapa 252	11'6"	5'2"	16.5"	121	1477	28
Mapa 302	12'6"	5'5"	17"	154	1577	40
Mapa 402	13'10"	6'3"	18"	196	2095	55
N-102	9'10"	4'5"	14"	55	937	7.5
N-202	11'0"	4'9"	15"	99	1135	20*
N-252	11'6"	5'2"	16.5"	108	1488	28
N-302	12'6"	5'5"	17"	148	1577	40

*Sailing equipment available as an optional extra.

MARAVIA (USA)

MARAVIA CORPORATION
857 Thornton Street,
P.O. Box 395,
San Leandro, CA 94577
(415) 483-2820

FABRIC TYPE: Polyester coated with PVC.

DINGHIES: Standard equipment — Bow ring, towing rings, fittings for bow dodger, rubbing strake, lifelines, fittings for outboard bracket, oars, oar retainers, inflatable thwart seat, pump, carrying bag, repair kit. Color: Light blue.

Cat's Paw	8'0"	4'0"	12"	37	500	3
Breeze	9'6"	4'10"	14"	42	950	4
Zephyr	12'0"	5'6"	16"	47	1200	6

SPORTBOATS: Standard equipment — Inflatable keel, marine plywood floorboards, bow ring, towing rings, fittings for bow dodger, rubbing strake, lifelines, oarlocks, oar retainers, inflatable thwart seat, carrying bag, repair kit.

Bora	10'6"	4'10"	14"	90	800	15
Tempest	12'6"	5'6"	16"	140	1200	35

RIVER BOATS: Standard equipment — Bow ring, heavy duty "D" rings (customer can specify placement), inflatable thwart seat(s), recessed valves, repair kit.

MODEL	LENGTH	BEAM	TUBE (DIA.)	WT. (LBS.)	CAP. (LBS.)	MAX. ENG H.P.
Elan	12'0"	5'9"	17"	70	1200	
Espirit	13'6"	6'0"	18"	95	1500	
Williwaw I	14'3"	6'8"	20"	110	2000	
Williwaw II	15'6"	7'6"	22"	105	2700	
Santana	15'6"	7'4"	21"	102	2650	
Mistral I	17'6"	8'0"	24"	150	3500	
Mistral II	17'6"	7'6"	20"	120	3200	
New River I	18'0"	8'0"	24"	150	3500	
New River II	20'6"	8'0"	24"	170	4200	

METZELER (Germany)

East Coast:
TRANS ATLANTIC AGENCIES, INC.
Suite 612, Keyser Bldg.,
Baltimore, MD 21202
(301) 837-6550

West Coast:
INFLATABLE BOAT CENTER
510 Santa Monica Blvd.
Santa Monica, CA 90401
(213) 395-8506

Canada:
IMPAX INTERNATIONAL LTD.
P.O. Box 35098
Vancouver, B.C. V6M 4G3

KAISER-DISTRIBUTORS LTD.
29 Advance Road
Toronto, Ontario M8Z 2S6

FABRIC TYPE: Polyester coated with a natural rubber/neoprene mixture overlayed with Hypalon.

DINGHIES: Standard equipment — Mooring/towing bridle, lifelines, outboard motor bracket, wooden seats (except Aztek), inflatable bottom, oarlocks, oars, oar retainers, fittings for sailing equipment (Aztek, Maya, Juca), pressure gauge, pump, carrying bag, repair kit. Color: Orange.

Tender II	8'9"	4'2"	13"	44	990	2
Tender I	9'6"	4'11"	15.5"	50	882	5
Aztek	9'2"	4'0"	13"	42	660	4*

MODEL	LENGTH	BEAM	TUBE (DIA.)	WT. (LBS.)	CAP. (LBS.)	MAX. ENG H.P.
Maya	10'11"	4'7"	14.5"	52	990	4*
Juca	12'10"	4'9"	14.5"	64	1100	6*

*Sailing equipment available as an optional extra.

CANOES and KAYAKS: Standard equipment — Varies with boat. All come equipped with pressure gauge, pump, carrying bag and repair kit. Spezi has a hanging fiberglass seat and ring for attaching spray skirt. Color: Orange.

Spezi L	14'5"	2'4"		46	282
Joker	11'6"	2'6"	8"	25	352
Tramper	12'2"	2'7"	9"	29	375
Riverstar	17'1"	2'9"	8.5"	64	660
Indio	14'7"	3'5"	9'	60	992

SPORTBOATS: Standard equipment — Inflatable keel, marine plywood floorboards, mooring and towing bridle, bow dodger (Esquire, Raystar), lifelines, self-bailers, pressure gauge, pump, carrying bag, repair kit. Brigant S and Markant S also come with oars, oar retainers, and fittings for sailing equipment.

Markant S	10'8"	4'11"	15.5"	104	880	12
Brigant S	12'8"	5'0"	16"	119	990	25
Elefant	14'5"	6'0"	17.5"	193	1320	55
Esquire S	12'6"	5'8"	15.5"	150	1100	28
Raystar LS	13'3"	3'3"	16"	165	1100	45

NORTHWEST RIVER SUPPLIES (Japan)

NORTHWEST RIVER SUPPLIES
214 North Main Street,
P.O. Box 9243,
Moscow, ID 83843
(208) 882-2383

FABRIC TYPE: Nylon coated with neoprene rubber.

RIVERBOATS: Standard equipment — Integral inflated thwart seats, recessed valves, rubbing strake, lifelines, "D" rings (Sport), repair kit. Color: Grey.

Sprite	11'2"	5'2"	16"	55	1500
Sport	14'9"	6'8"	20"	100	3000

NOVURANIA (Italy)

PROKO INTERNATIONAL
12511 Beatrice Street,
Los Angeles, CA 90066
(213) 391-6391

FABRIC TYPE: Polyester coated with neoprene/Hypalon mixture.

DINGHIES: Standard equipment — Bow ring, rubbing strake, lifelines, fitting for outboard bracket (Poseidon Dinghy), transom (Pram), oars, oar retainers, pump, carrying bag, repair kit. Colors: Yellow, orange or grey.

MODEL	LENGTH	BEAM	TUBE (DIA.)	WT. (LBS.)	CAP. (LBS.)	MAX. ENG H.P.
Poseidon Dinghy	8'4"	4'6"	13"	44	550	5
Canguro Pram	8'0"	4'10"	15"	88	425	12

SPORTBOATS: Standard equipment — Wooden keel, marine plywood floorboards, bow handle, bow dodger, rubbing strake, lifelines, oars, oar retainers, self-bailers, lifting handles, pump, carrying bag, repair kit. Colors: Yellow, orange or grey.

NOVURANIA sportboats come in two models:
Canguro series have a deep "V" hull, gull-wing stern and wider beam.
Poseidon models have greater draft, larger diameter hull tubes.

MODEL	LENGTH	BEAM	TUBE (DIA.)	WT. (LBS.)	CAP. (LBS.)	MAX. ENG H.P.
Canguro 2	9'5"	5'1"	15"	111	625	20
Canguro 3	10'2"	5'6"	17"	130	800	30
Canguro 4	11'0"	5'6"	17"	161	900	40
Canguro 5	12'8"	6'0"	18"	191	1125	55
Canguro 6	13'7"	6'1"	18.5"	209	1250	60
Poseidon 1	10'2"	4'9"	15"	114	725	20
Poseidon 2	11'6"	5'3"	17"	149	1000	30
Poseidon 3	12'4"	5'7"	18.5"	182	1250	40
Poseidon 4	14'3"	6'3"	21"	226	1775	55
Poseidon 6	16'0"	7'0"	22"	338	2222	65

PYRAWA (France)

LEISURE IMPORTS, INC.
104 Arlington Avenue,
St. James, NY 11780
(516) 724-8900

FABRIC TYPES: Unsupported PVC. Color: Orange and PVC supported by wide-mesh polyester fibers (Explorer series). Color: Silver.

KAYAKS/CANOES: "Sea Eagle" sport canoes, and "Sea Eagle Explorer" canoes.

MODEL	LENGTH	BEAM	TUBE (DIA.)	WT. (LBS.)	CAP. (LBS.)	MAX. ENG H.P.
SE-290	9'8"	2'9"		19	400	
SE-330	11'2"	2'9"		23	500	
Explorer Series						
SE-300X	9'6"	2'9"		27	450	
SE-340X	11'0"	2'9"		34	600	
SE-380X	12'5"	2'9"		36	750	

DINGHIES: "Sea Eagle" and "Sea Eagle Explorer" dinghies.

SE-3	5'8"	3'3"		8	250	
SE-4	6'8"	4'0"		12	350	
SE-5	7'4"	4'2"		14	450	
SE-6	8'8"	4'4"		20	750	2
SE-8	9'7"	4'6"		31	950	2
SE-9	11'0"	4'8"		40	1200	2
Explorer Series						
SE VII-X	7'10"	4'2"		29	650	3
SE VIII-X	9'8"	4'8"		38	1000	5

ROGUE INFLATABLES (Japan)

ROGUE INFLATABLES, INC.
P.O. Box 266,
Grants Pass, OR 97526
(503) 476-3027

FABRIC TYPE: Nylon coated with neoprene/Hypalon mixture.

RIVERBOATS: Standard equipment — Bow ring, "D" rings for attaching rowing frame, integral thwart seats, recessed valves, rubbing strake. Color: International orange.

Illinois	11'6"	5'8"	16"	115	1700
McKenzie	14'9"	6'9"	18.7"	150	3000
Rogue	17'8"	7'11"	21.5"	175	4000

215

RUBBER CRAFTERS (USA)

RUBBER CRAFTERS OF WEST VIRGINIA, INC.
Route 47,
P.O. Box 8,
Smithville, WV 26178
(304) 477-3342

FABRIC TYPE: Nylon coated with neoprene rubber.

RIVERBOATS: Standard equipment — "D" rings, recessed valves, inflatable thwart seats. NOTE: The Salmon and Colorado boats are commercial rigs usually made to the specifications of the outfitter.

MODEL	LENGTH	BEAM	TUBE (DIA.)	WT. (LBS.)	CAP. (LBS.)	MAX. ENG H.P.
Lehigh	11'0"	5'6"	15"		not provided	
Voyageur	12'0"	5'6"	16"		not provided	
Potomac	14'0"	7'0"	18"		not provided	
Yampa	15'0"	7'0"	18"		not provided	
Green River	16'6"	8'0"	18"		not provided	
Grand	18'4"	8'0"	22"		not provided	
Salmon	16 to 24'	8'0"	24"		not provided	
Colorado	22 to 37'	9'0"	36"		not provided	

SEMPERIT (Austria)

STEYR DAIMLER PUCH OF AMERICA CORPORATION
80 Field Point Road,
P.O. Box 7777,
Greenwich, CT 06830
(203) 661-2202

FABRIC TYPE: Nylon or polyester (depending on model) coated with a natural rubber/neoprene mixture and overlayed with Hypalon.

DINGHIES: Standard equipment — Bow ring (except Siesta), outboard bracket (except Siesta), lifelines, inflatable bottom (except D-250), oarlocks, fittings for sailing equipment (Venecia I and II only). The D-250 also includes the following items: wooden seat and marine plywood floorboards. Color: Yellow.

Siesta	6'10"	3'3"	11.5"	18	440	
Venecia I	9'2"	4'3"	14"	31	880	2*
Venecia II	10'10"	4'3"	14"	40	1320	2*
D-250	8'4"	4'8"	13.5"	51	660	4

*Sailing equipment available as an optional extra.

CANOES and KAYAKS: Standard equipment — Wooden stem piece, bow and stern dodgers, fittings for rudders and sails (Forelle II), backrest(s). Color: Yellow.

MODEL	LENGTH	BEAM	TUBE (DIA.)	WT. (LBS.)	CAP. (LBS.)	MAX. ENG H.P.
Forelle II	12'0"	2'3"	6.5"	26	660*	
Forelle III	13'1"	2'3"	5"	33	704	
Dolphin II**	12'0"	2'3"	6.5"	37	660	

*Sailing equipment available as an optional extra.
**The Dolphin II is a specially adapted version of the Forelle II for river running. It was designed by Helmuth Peters of the Inflatable Boat Center (see Metzeler listing) and is imported by his company.

SAILBOATS: All sailboats come fully equipped for sailing. Color: Yellow. NOTE: In addition to the boats which have been specially designed for sailing, sailing equipment is available as an optional extra to convert the following boats to that purpose: Venecia I and II, Forelle II, A-330, Hecht L, Speed L and Sprinter GTL.

Wasserfloh	7'3"	2'11"		29	220
Semper Surf***	9'8"	2'8"		53	440
Kat 360	11'4"	5'8"	16"	106	660
Kat 416	13'1"	6'9"	16"	128	990
Kat 516	15'5"	7'6"	18"	220	1760

***The Semper Surf is a stand-up windsurfer.

SPORTBOATS: Standard equipment — Wooden keel, marine plywood floorboards, bow handle, lifting handles (except Speed L), oarlocks, bow dodger (except A-330 and Hecht L). Color: Yellow.

A-330	10'9"	4'11"	14.5"	99	814	15*
Hecht L	10'2"	4'7"	15.5"	88	990	10*
Speed L	10'2"	4'6"	14"	90	770	10*
Sprinter GTL	11'1"	4'11"	15.5"	121	1100	25*
Feuerpfeil GTL	13'1"	5'9"	17.5"	123	1540	45
Sonny 350***	12'2"	5'4"	16.5"	224	1056	35

*Sailing equipment available as an optional extra.
***The Sonny 350 has a six piece "V" shaped inner wooden bottom which, in effect, creates a hard lower hull similar to the fiberglass bottom on Hybrid boats.

SEVYLOR (France)

East Coast:
SEVYLOR
213 Louisville Air Park,
Louisville, KY 40213
(502) 361-1676

West Coast:
SEVYLOR
6802 E. Watcher Street,
Los Angeles, CA 90040
(213) 927-3473

FABRIC TYPE: PVC.

Sevylor offers a wide selection of inflatables, some of which are expressly designed for children. The latter are not included in the following listings.

KAYAKS: The "Tahiti" and the "Tahiti Sport" series:

MODEL	LENGTH	BEAM	TUBE (DIA.)	WT. (LBS.)	CAP. (LBS.)	MAX. ENG H.P.
K-67/K-69	9'6"	2'8"		18/27	280	
K-77	10'8"	2'10"		21	380	
K-79	11'0"	2'10"		31	380	

DINGHIES: The "Caravelle" series, models K-76 through K-126, can be equipped with a motor mount, sailing rig, or a canopy sun roof.

MODEL	LENGTH	BEAM	TUBE (DIA.)	WT. (LBS.)	CAP. (LBS.)	MAX. ENG H.P.
K-36	5'5"	3'9"		8	275	
K-56	6'5"	3'10"		15	450	
K-66	7'3"	4'3"		18	600	
K-76	8'0"	4'4"		27	680	3*
K-86	9'0"	4'4"		29	700	3*
K-106	10'0"	4'8"		33	940	3*
K-116	11'2"	4'8"		41	1120	3*
K-126	12'0"	4'8"		45	1200	3*

SPORTBOATS: Standard equipment — Inflatable keel, marine plywood floorboards, bow handle, bow dodger, rubbing strake, oarlocks, oar retainers, carrying bag, repair kit. Color: White.

MODEL	LENGTH	BEAM	TUBE (DIA.)	WT. (LBS.)	CAP. (LBS.)	MAX. ENG H.P.
K-68	9'0"	4'8"		81	390	6*
K-88	11'0"	5'3"		110	590	10*

*Sailing equipment available as an optional extra.

ZODIAC (France)

East Coast:
ZODIAC OF NORTH AMERICA, INC.
11 Lee Street,
Annapolis, MD 21401
(301) 268-2009

West Coast:
ZODIAC WEST
1275 Railroad St.,
Corona, CA 91720
(714) 734-3780

FABRIC TYPES: ZED models: Polyester coated with PVC. Regular models: Nylon coated with neoprene/Hypalon mixture.

ZED MODELS

DINGHIES and SPORT DINGHIES: Standard equipment — Towing bridle, lifelines, oars, oar retainers, slatted floorboards (ZED 4), self-bailer (ZED 4), pump, carrying bag, repair kit. Color: Red-orange.

MODEL	LENGTH	BEAM	TUBE (DIA.)	WT. (LBS.)	CAP. (LBS.)	MAX. ENG H.P.
ZED 2	6'6"	4'0"	13.5"	20	550	2
ZED 4	8'2"	4'8"	15"	40	925	4

SPORTBOATS: Standard equipment — Inflatable keel, marine plywood floorboards, bow ring, painter, bow dodger (except 26), rubbing strake, lifelines, oars, oar retainers, self-bailers, pump, carrying bag, repair kit. Color: Beige.

MODEL	LENGTH	BEAM	TUBE (DIA.)	WT. (LBS.)	CAP. (LBS.)	MAX. ENG H.P.
ZED 26	8'2"	4'8"	15"	62	925	4
ZED 31	10'2"	4'8"	not provided	73	1000	10
ZED 34	11'3"	5'6"	not provided	93	1300	20

REGULAR MODELS

DINGHIES: Standard equipment — Bow ring or towing rings, painter, rubbing strake, life lines (except YouYou), oars, pump, carrying bag, repair kit. Color: Grey.

MODEL	LENGTH	BEAM	TUBE (DIA.)	WT. (LBS.)	CAP. (LBS.)	MAX. ENG H.P.
Youyou	7'3"	3'8"	12"	33	505	4
Tender IV	9'2"	4'7"	14"	48	880	4
Tender VI	10'2"	4'8"	13"	55	950	4
Dinghy 1507*	9'6"	5'3"		88	1000	4

*See listing under Part II: LIFERAFTS.

SPORTBOATS: Standard equipment — Inflatable keel, marine plywood or aluminum floorboards (depending on model), bow ring or handle, painter, bow dodger (except Cadet and Mark V), rubbing strake, lifelines, oars or paddles (Mark IV and V), oar retainers, self-bailers, lifting handles (Mark I Deluxe and larger), Anti-splash vanes (except Cadet, Mark I Junior and Mark V), mast and pennant (most models), pump, carrying bag, repair kit. Colors: GT boats - Orange and black; Mark V - Black; all other boats - Grey.

ZODIAC sportboats come in five models:

Lightweight grey boats that can double as tenders.

Standard boats that are grey and have wooden floorboards.

GT boats with aluminum floorboards.

Grand Raid (GR) boats which have aluminum floorboards, heavier hardware and reinforced hull and black trim.

Mark V Heavy Duty workboat.

MODEL	LENGTH	BEAM	TUBE (DIA.)	WT. (LBS.)	CAP. (LBS.)	MAX. ENG H.P.
Lightweight Boats						
Cadet	9'10"	4'8"	14"	64	825	10
Mark I, Junior	10'6"	4'10"	16"	97	880	10
Standard Boats						
Mark I, Deluxe	10'6"	4'10"	16"	111	880	25
Mark II Compact	12'6"	5'6"	18"	147	1320	40
Mark II	13'10"	5'6"	18"	170	1500	55
Mark III	15'5"	6'4"	20"	211	2400	65
GT Boats						
Mark II Compact GT	12'6"	5'6"	18"	161	1320	40
Mark II GT	13'10"	5'6"	18"	176	1500	55
Grand Raid Boats						
Mark II GR	13'10"	5'6"	18"	178	1500	55
Mark III GR	15'5"	6'4"	20"	247	2400	65
Mark IV GR	17'6"	7'2"	22"	297	2750	85 L/Shaft
Mark V Heavy Duty	19'6"	8'5"	25"	465	3970	2 X 55 L/Shaft

PART II: LIFERAFTS

Note: When the term "Canister" is used it refers to the fiberglass container regardless of shape.

AVON INFLATABLES LIMITED (England)

North and Southeastern States:
IMTRA CORPORATION
151 Mystic Avenue,
Medford, MA 02155
(617) 391-5660

Midwest and Central Eastern States:
INLAND MARINE COMPANY
79 East Jackson Street,
Wilkes-Barre, PA 18701
(717) 822-7185

Western States, Texas, Alaska:
SEAGULL MARINE
1851 McGaw Avenue,
Irvine, CA 92714
(714) 979-6161

Canada:
AVON INFLATABLES OF CANADA LTD.
1410 Spears Road,
Oakville, Ontario L6L 5M1
(416) 827-6919

LIFERAFTS: Standard equipment — Available in either fiberglass pack or nylon valise. Automatic lanyard activated CO-2 inflation, self-erecting canopy, stabilizing pockets, sea-activated light, survival equipment kit, blow off/topping up valves, inner and outer lifelines, double inflatable floor model available for temperate and cold climate use.

MODEL	WEIGHT	VALISE: LENGTH/ DIAMETER	CANISTER: LENGTH/ WIDTH/HEIGHT
4 Person	63/72*	25" × 15"	32" × 19" × 12"
6 Person	82/93*	28" × 16"	33" × 23" × 12"
8 Person	94/106*	28" × 16"	33" × 23" × 12"
10 Person	106/118*	28" × 16"	33" × 23" × 12"

*Weight of valise/fiberglass pack model.

GIVENS BUOY LIFERAFT

RES-Q-RAFT, INC.
152 Common Fence Blvd.,
Portsmouth, RI 02871
(401) 683-3822

LIFERAFTS: Standard equipment — Available in either fiberglass container or fabric valise. Automatic lanyard operated CO-2 nitrogen inflation, self-erecting canopy, large stabilizing chamber, deballasting line, sea activated light, survival equipment kit, inner and outer boarding ladder, interior safety strap, double floor, double canopy (Deluxe rafts only).

The GIVENS BUOY RAFT is available in four models:
6 Man Deluxe Model A has double floor, double canopy, full survival kit.
6 Man Model B has double floor, single canopy, limited survival kit.
6 Man Sea Sail has single floor, single canopy, limited survival kit.
8 Man Deluxe Offshore Raft has double floor, double canopy, full survival kit.

MODEL	WEIGHT	VALISE: LENGTH/ WIDTH/HEIGHT	CANISTER: LENGTH/ WIDTH/HEIGHT
Deluxe Model A	87/120*	34" × 17" × 15"	30.5" × 16.3" × 16"
Model B	57/90*	34" × 17" × 15"	30.5" × 16.3" × 16"
Sea Snail	52/85*	34" × 17" × 15"	30.5" × 16.3" × 16"
8 Man Deluxe	97/130*	35" × 24.3" × 14"	39.5" × 25" × 15"

*Weight of valise/canister model.

RFD-PATTEN LIFE RAFTS (England)

RFD-PATTEN, INC.
1803 Madrid Avenue,
P.O. Box 31
Lake Worth, FL 33461
(305) 588-8500

LIFERAFTS: Standard equipment — Available in either fiberglass container* or fabric valise. Automatic lanyard activated CO-2 inflation, stabilizing pockets, self-erecting canopy*, sea-activated light*, survival equipment kit, lifelines, ladder, topping up valves.
*except on Seafly models.

RFD-PATTEN liferafts are available in three models:
Seafly 4/6 man models designed for aviation use.
Seasava 4 man circular liferaft.
6 man six sided raft.

MODEL	WEIGHT	VALISE: LENGTH/ WIDTH/HEIGHT	CANISTER: LENGTH/ WIDTH/HEIGHT
Seafly 4/6 Man	22	24.5″ × 13.7″ × 16.3″	Not available in canister
Seasava 4 Man	34	27″ × 12″ × 9″	No data available
6 Man Liferaft	68/80*	30.1″ × 15.1″ × 10.6″	33.7″ × 11.2″ × 17.7″

*Weight of valise/canister model.

SEA-JAY ELLIOT YFC LIFERAFTS (USA)

C.J. HENDRY COMPANY
139 Townsend Street,
San Francisco, CA 94107
(415) 362-4242

LIFERAFTS: Standard equipment — Available in fiberglass container or fabric valise. Automatic lanyard activated CO-2 inflation, self-erecting canopy, stabilizing pockets, sea activated light, survival equipment kit, inner and outer lifelines, boarding handgrips. Inflatable floor insert available for temperate and cold climate use.

MODEL	VALISE DIMENSIONS	CANISTER: LENGTH/WIDTH/HEIGHT
4 Man	64/82* See below**	24″ × 23.5″ × 13″
6 Man	81/98* See below**	37.5″ × 25″ × 15″
8 Man	82/107* See below**	42″ × 23.5″ × 13″
10 Man	92/120* See below**	45.5″ × 25″ × 16.5″

*Weight of valise/canister model. Can vary with equipment enclosed.
**Valise may be 1 to 3 inches smaller than fiberglass container.

SWITLIK INFLATABLE LIFERAFTS

SWITLICK PARACHUTE COMPANY, INC.
1325 East State Street,
Trenton, NJ 08607
(609) 587-3300

LIFERAFTS: Standard equipment — All Switlik liferafts are U.S. Coast Guard approved. Available in fiberglass canister only. Automatic lanyard activated CO-2 inflation, stabilizing pockets, self-erecting canopy (insulated), insulated floor, sea activated light, survival equipment kit, lifelines, ladder, sea anchor, topping up/pressure relief valves, inflating and bilge pump, (all rafts except the four man come with survival equipment for either limited or ocean service. Ocean service kit contains all limited equipment plus augmenting supplies).

Note: In addition to the survival rafts listed, Switlik also offers rafts for 15, 20 and 25 men. Since these are intended for commercial applications the specification are not included in this group.

MODEL	WEIGHT	DIMENSIONS: DIAMETER X LENGTH
4 Man	210	18″ dia. × 39″
6 Man	240/290*	21″ dia. × 44″
8 Man	270/320*	21″ dia. × 44″
10 Man	300/355*	24″ dia. × 49″

*Weight of limited pack/ocean pack.

WINSLOW LIFERAFTS (USA)

WINSLOW COMPANY
928 S. Tamiami Trail,
P.O. Box 578,
Osprey, FL 33559
(813) 966-2114

LIFERAFTS: Standard equipment — Available in fiberglass container or fabric valise. Automatic lanyard activated CO-2 inflation, self-erecting canopy (MCR and CRR models only), hand holds. CRR has the following additional equipment: self-erecting canopy, stabilizing pockets, boarding ladder, exterior/interior lifelines.

WINSLOW LIFERAFTS are available in three models:
M Series - open oblong rafts in 2, 4, 6, 8, 10, 12 man sizes.
MCR Series - Oblong rafts with radar reflecting canopy. (Same size as M series.)
CRR Series - Circular rafts with radar reflecting canopy in 4, 6, 8, 10, 12 man sizes.

MODEL	WEIGHT	VALISE: LENGTH/ WIDTH/	CANISTER: LENGTH/ WIDTH/HEIGHT
2 Man M and MCR	18/28*	23″ × 10″ × 8″	16″ × 20″ × 30.5″
4 Man M and MCR	30/42*	25″ × 11″7.5″	as above
6 Man M and MCR	32/45*	29″ × 13″ × 7.5″	as above
8 Man M and MCR	38/50*	30″ × 14″ × 8″	as above

THE COMPLETE BOOK OF
Inflatable Boats

CDR DON HUBBARD, USN (Ret)

$7.95

5½" x 8½" / Paperback
256 pages / $7.95

THE COMPLETE BOOK OF

INFLATABLE BOATS

CDR Don Hubbard, USN(Ret)

A consumer guide that tells how to buy a small tough boat with the capability of a much larger one for scuba diving, river running, water skiing, canoeing, kayaking yacht tender or sailing. This unique hand book, the only one of its kind, is packed with detailed information on the design and construction of every type of inflatable with data on their use and care. Nearly 400 models available in the U.S. are fully described with technical specifications with almost 100 photos and diagrams.

LANDFALLS
OF PARADISE

The Guide to Pacific Islands
Earl R. Hinz

This is the only book of its kind, devoted to getting around the Pacific, particularly in your own boat. Detailed descriptions are presented for each of the 33 island groups covering geography, history and native society. Planning information includes weather, Ports of Entry, immigration procedures, yacht facilities and supplie language, currency, health and communications. It is broadly divided in Polynesia, Melanesia and Micronesia. Anyone planning or simply dreaming a trip to the "Paradise Islands" will find this invaluable. 143 photos plus over hundred specially drawn two-color charts. Index and glossary. A Selection the Dolphin Book Club.

8½" x 11" / Hardcover — Intro. Price: $24.95
After Jan. 1, 1981: $29.95

Royce's
SAILING ILLUSTRATED
7th Revised Edition

A world-wide best seller since 1956 is now available in a new enlarged edition. The larger format (Reader's Digest size) is easier to read, has dozens of new pages packed with up-to-the minute data on learning to sail, racing rules, Olympic classes, Rules of the Road, navigational lights, safety procedures, etc., etc.

A must for every sailer and boat owner. It's used by sailing schools all over the world. A whole new generation of sailors are discovering this classic.

5" x 7½". 352 pages / $7.95

Pat Royce's
TRAILERBOATING ILLUSTRATED

A handbook about portable boats up to 30 feet, especially those with planing capabilities. How to choose the hull, the motor and the trailer are all covered in this new, easily-understood manual.

Pat Royce, a leader in boating education better known for his best-selling **SAILING ILLUSTRATED**, provides the most needed and often the most difficult answers concerning the trailerboat in this first volume of a series. Several hundred illustrations.

6" x 9" Paperback. 192 pages / $5.95

MARINE RADIO
PROCEDURES GUIDE

How to be an expert with your marine radio. This easy-to-use guide for ship-to-ship and ship-to-shore calls is prepared by Ken Englert, editor of the popular electronics column in BOATING MAGAZINE. A concise interpretation of the complex VHF rules including step-by-step operating procedures and vital distress information. Printed on two sides. Mounted in heavy, weatherproof plastic.

8½" x 11" / $2.95

Order Form

•1980 PACIFIC BOATING ALMANACS
_____ Southern California, Arizona, Baja edition / 6.95
_____ Northern California & Nevada edition / 6.95
_____ Pacific Northwest edition / 6.95

•ROYCE PUBLICATIONS
_____ Sailing Illustrated / 7.95
_____ Sailing Illustrated Workbook / 2.95
_____ Trailerboating Illustrated-1: Planing Hulls-
Trailers-Seamanship / 5.95

•CLYMER BOATING MAINTENANCE HANDBOOKS
_____ Sailboat Maintenance / 9.00
_____ Powerboat Maintenance / 9.00
_____ British Seagull Outboards / 8.00
_____ Chrysler Outboards (3.5 to 20 HP) / 8.00
_____ Chrysler Outboards (25 to 135 HP) / 8.00
_____ Evinrude Outboards (1.5 to 35 HP) / 8.00
_____ Evinrude Outboards (40 to 140 HP) / 8.00
_____ Johnson Outboards (1.5 to 35 HP) / 8.00
_____ Johnson Outboards (40 to 140 HP) / 8.00
_____ Mercury Outboards (4 to 40 HP) / 8.00
_____ Mercury Outboards (50 to 175 HP) / 8.00
_____ Stern Drive Service / 9.00

•OTHER SELECT MARINE BOOKS
_____ Complete Book of Inflatable Boats / 7.95
_____ Cruising Guide to Channel Islands / 16.95
_____ Exploring the Coast by Boat - B.C. & Wash. / 8.95
_____ Exploring the Seashore - B.C., Wash. & Oregon / 9.95
_____ Landfalls of Paradise - Guide to Pac. Islands / 24.95
_____ Northwest Passages-I / 8.95
_____ 141 Dives in Protected Waters of Wash. & B.C. / 9.95
_____ Pac. Coast Inshore Fishes / 10.95
_____ Pac. Coast Nudibranchs / 14.95
_____ Pac. Coast Subtidal Marine Invertebrates / 9.50
_____ VHF Radio Procedures Guide (Laminated) / 2.95
_____ Southeastern Alaska / 5.95
_____ 1980 Spyglass / 5.95

•TIDAL CURRENT CHARTS (Laminated)
_____ Puget Sound, Southern Part / 5.95
_____ Puget Sound, Northern Part / 5.95
_____ San Francisco Bay / 5.95

Send order to your neighborhood bookstore, marine store, or
Western Marine Enterprises, Inc., Box Q, Ventura, CA 93002

☐ Rush the books checked above.
Check or money order is enclosed.

_____ Sub total

___$1.25___ Shipping charge per order

_____ California Residents add 6% sales tax

Ship to: (Name and complete address)

_____

_____

_____ Zip_____

• Money Back Guarantee
If not completely satisfied, return your order within 10 days for a full refund.

Note: Prices listed here are in effect June 1980 and are subject to change without notice. In Canada, order from Gordon Soules, 525-355 Burrard St., Vancouver, B.C. V6C 2G8. Prices in Canada are generally higher than U.S. prices.

MODEL	WEIGHT	VALISE: LENGTH/ WIDTH/HEIGHT	CANISTER: LENGTH/ WIDTH/HEIGHT
10 Man M and MCR	42/60*	30" × 14" × 8"	16" × 20" × 30.5"
12 Man M and MCR	52/64*	30" × 18.5" × 11"	as above
4 Man CRR	75	not available	as above
6 Man CRR	85	not available	as above
8 Man CRR	87	not available	as above
10 Man CRR	90	not available	as above
12 Man CRR	92	not available	as above

*Weight of valise/canister models. MCR Series weight slightly more.

ZODIAC LIFERAFTS (France)

ZODIAC OF NORTH AMERICA, INC.
11 Lee Street,
Annapolis, MD 21401
(301) 268-2009

LIFERAFTS: Standard equipment* — Available in fiberglass container or fabric valise. Automatic lanyard activated CO_2 inflation, stabilizing pockets, self-erecting canopy (except SY-6 is manual), interior/exterior lifelines, survival equipment kit. MP 6 also includes the following items: boarding ladder, interior/exterior seawater activated lights, overpressure relief valve. MPS has inflatable double bottom.

*Zodiac 1507 dinghy/liferaft standard equipment as follows: Manually operated CO_2, manually erected canopy with supports, waterproof pouch fitted to bow, sculling fitting on transom, righting handle, interior/exterior lifelines, bellows, 2 hand pumps, oars, bailer, survival equipment kit.

ZODIAC LIFERAFTS are available in four models:

6, 8 or 10 man MPS raft — square shape, double inflatable bottom, very complete survival kit.

6 man MP raft — square shape, somewhat reduced survival kit.

6 man SY raft — pentagonal shape, manually operated canopy, somewhat reduced survival kit. Designed for near-shore yachting.

Model 1507 dinghy/liferaft — a specially designed dinghy equipped with CO_2 manual inflation for emergencies and other items listed above. Boat can be used as a survival raft or yacht tender.

MODEL	WEIGHT	VALISE: LENGTH/ WIDTH/HEIGHT	CANISTER: LENGTH/ WIDTH/HEIGHT
MPS 6 Man	105.8/116.9*	31″ × 19″ × 11.5″	31″ × 20″ × 12″
MPS 8 Man	141.1/154.3*	35″ × 20.5″ × 13″	35″ × 21.5″ × 14″
MPS 10 Man	165.4/180.8*	36″ × 20″ × 13″	38″ × 22″ × 14″
MP 6 Man	68/77*	32″ × 20″ × 16″	33″ × 21″ × 12″
SY 6 Man	46.3/47.4*	27″ × 16″ × 7″	28″ × 16″ × 7″
Dinghy 1507	88.2	43″ × 15.5″ × 14″	Not available

*Weight of valise/canister model.

Appendices

APPENDIX I
Inflatable Boat Buyer's Checklist

Type of boat	Cost
Length	Beam

Weight in bags	Number of chambers
Size in bags	Tube diameter
Rated capacity	Hull material
(Weight & persons)	Normal operating pressure
Engine rating	
*Type keel	

EQUIPMENT SUPPLIED	FITTINGS — NOTE STRENGTH AND QUALITY
Instruction booklet	Bow eye or handle
Pump	Lifelines
Carrying bags	"D" rings
Repair kit	Towing rings
Pressure gauge	Carrying handles
Oars	Oarlocks
Bow dodger	*Anti-hogging strips (Boats rated at 30 H.P. or more)
Seats	*Wheel mounting brackets
**Outboard bracket	*Self-bailing device

INVESTIGATE:

Warranty: Note exclusions, time limits, deductibles, where boat must be sent.

Valves: Corrosion resistant, ease of operation, large enough to deflate easily.

Woodwork: Good quality, well-crafted, well-finished, light in weight.

Workmanship: Clean, neat and even seams, fittings properly positioned. Ease of assembly and disassembly.

Dealer network: For warranty claims, spare parts, accessories.

*Sportboats only
**Dinghies only

APPENDIX II

List of Suggested Equipment for Inflatable Boats
Used in Rescue Service
(Select as required)

Anchor and line

Blankets

Boarding ladder

Boat hook

Bull horn

Compass and charts with
beach coordinates

Dry storage bags

Exposure suits

Fire extinguisher

First aid equipment

Flag: high visibility on
tall mast

Flares and signaling devices

Flashlight

Launching wheels

Oars and spares

Padding for deck

Personal flotation devices

Pump and hose

Radio: Two way portable,
waterproof marine

"RESCUE" (Painted on sides
in large letters)

Resuscitation equipment

Propeller guard

Running lights

Sea anchor

Self-bailing device

Skin diving equipment
(mask, snorkel, fins)

Spare fuel tank

Strobe light

Throwing devices and line

Tools for engine

Towing bridle and tow line

Trailing line with hand grips or
knots (100 ')

Urinal

APPENDIX III
Supplementary Survival Equipment List
(Select as required — pack in a waterproof container)

FOR SIGNALING

Signaling mirror

Radar reflector

Emergency marine radio
equipment

Flashing strobe light

Signal flares — day

Signal flares — night

Dye marker

Flashlight and spare batteries

Whistle

FOOD AND WATER

Solar water distillation kit
(one for two persons —
minimum)

Canned water

Canned lifeboat rations

Multi-vitamins

HEALTH AND COMFORT

First aid kit

Sunscreen lotion

Anti-seasickness pills

Plastic bailer and urinal

Knife and sharpening stone

Spare nylon line

Waterproof matches

Cutting board

Plastic bags

Bailing sponge

Sea anchor

Space blanket

Survival literature

Raft repair kit

Raft leak stoppers

Vaseline

Can opener

Fishing equipment — 400 feet of 50 pound test line, 40 non-rusting hooks, steel wire leaders with attaching snaps, 20 small lead sinkers, spoons with treble hooks, feathered jigs, extra snaps for attaching hooks.

NOTE: The above equipment should be packaged in a buoyant waterproof container and stowed where it will be accessible in an emergency. The package should be brightly marked and should have a secure lanyard attached so that it can be secured to your survival raft.

If additional water is desired, stow it in partly full plastic bottles to provide flotation. Check the contents periodically to insure freshness.

APPENDIX IV
Sources of Supply for Specialty Equipment

In general the following suppliers are wholesalers who only deal with established businesses. The list is intended to serve as a guide for your dealer so that he will be able to obtain accessory items for you which may not be available through his own inflatable boat distributor. Since this list is not intended to be exhaustive, your dealer may already have better sources for some of the items listed. The publisher welcomes corrections and/or additions so that future editions will be able to be more comprehensive.

ADHESIVES (for neoprene/Hypalon hulls)
>Neoprene Adhesive F-1
>Carboline Company
>350 Hanley Industrial Court
>St. Louis, MO 63144
>(314) 644-1000

ADHESIVES (for Poly Vinyl Chloride hulls)
>Jet Set V
>Speedo Magic, Incorporated
>1837 Decatur Street
>Ridgewood, Queens, NY 11227
>(212) 366-6518

ANTI-THEFT DEVICE (for neoprene/Hypalon hulls)
>Avon Inflatables Limited
>(Three U.S. distributors)
>See listing under AVON, Chapter 7

ARMOR ALL
>Very Important Products, Inc.
>P.O. Box 7190
>Newport Beach, CA 92660
>(714) 833-2574

BAIT TANKS AND PUMPS
>Aquasea, Inc.
>1733 Monrovia Avenue
>Costa Mesa, CA 92627
>(714) 645-6180

CANVAS BOW DODGERS AND BOAT COVERS
Golden Fleece Designs
441 S. Victory Blvd.
Burbank, CA 91502
(213) 848-7724

COATING MATERIALS (for neoprene/Hypalon hulls)
Gaco Western, Inc.
P.O. Box 88698
Seattle, WA 98188
(206) 575-0450

Pacific Marine Development
10424 Empire Way
Seattle, WA 98178
(206) 722-8090

DECK COVERING
Rubbermaid Anti-Fatigue Matting #1814

Rubbermaid Commercial Products, Inc.
Eastern Division
3124 Valley Avenue
Winchester, VA 22601
(703) 667-8700

Western Division
2801 Junipero, Suite 206
Long Beach, CA 90805
(213) 595-4441

DOEL FIN
Doelcher Products, Inc.
P.O. Box 5215
Mission Hills, CA 91345
(213) 368-6525

DRY STORAGE BAGS
California Rivers
P.O. Box 468
Geyserville, CA 95441
(707) 857-3872

DRY STORAGE BAGS (Continued)

Northwest River Supplies
P.O. Box 9243
Moscow, ID 83843
(208) 882-2383

Phoenix Products
U.S. Route 421
Tyner, KY 40486
(502) 364-5141

Voyageurs Ltd.
P.O. Box 512
Shawnee Mission, KS 66201
(913) 262-6611

FUEL TANKS, FLEXIBLE

W.H. Den Ouden Co.
7170 Standard Drive
Dorsey, MD 21076
(301) 796-4740

Seagull Marine
1851 McGaw Avenue
Irvine, CA 92714
(714) 979-6161

Zodiac of North America
11 Lee Street
Annapolis, MD 21401
(301) 268-2009

JET DRIVE CONVERSION UNITS

Specialty Manufacturing Company
2035 Edison Avenue
San Leandro, CA 94577
(415) 562-6049

LAUNCHING WHEELS

Bodge Engineering
5047 Sixth Street
Carpenteria, CA 93013
(805) 684-5950

Bonair Boats
15501 West 109th Street
Lenexa, KS 66219
(913) 888-8484

Load-A-Boat
14912 N.E. 31st Circle
Redmond, WA 98052
(206) 883-6726

Proko International (Novurania Boats)
12511 Beatrice Street
Los Angeles, CA 90066
(213) 391-6391

Zodiac of North America
11 Lee Street
Annapolis, MD 21401
(301) 268-2009

SCUBA TANK RACKS

Pelican Products
23763 Madison Street
Torrance, CA 90505
(213) 373-7358

SEATING (Fiberglass Bass Boat Seats, Swivel Seats and Fittings)

Garelick Manufacturing Company
Saint Paul Park, MN 55071
(612) 459-9795

SEATING (Gas Tank Box Seats)

Ocean Ventures
966 Felspar Avenue
San Diego, CA 92109
(714) 272-3131

Proko International
12511 Beatrice Street
Los Angeles, CA 90066
(213) 391-6391

Zodiac of North America
11 Lee Street
Annapolis, MD 21401
(301) 268-2009

SELF-BAILING DEVICES

DePersia
P.O. Box 192
Grand Haven, MI 49417
(616) 842-1240

Tempo Products Company
6200 Cochran Road
Cleveland, OH 44139
(216) 248-1450

APPENDIX V
Some Information About Hypalon

The DuPont trademarked word HYPALON has been one of the most used and abused in the inflatable boat industry. The material is a synthetic rubber consisting of chlorosulfonated polyethylene, and in DuPont's words, it is ". . . a vulcanizable elastomer with a broad range of useful properties." This can certainly be the case, but DuPont also makes another point quite clear. Proper compounding is essential. In the DuPont pamphlet, ENGINEERING PROPERTIES OF DUPONT HYPALON, the following caveat is set forth on page 1:

"When you have reached the final page of this report, you will have read the words 'properly compounded' exactly 22 times. Why these words are so important in a discussion of the properties of HYPALON is covered in the paragraphs below. We urge you to read this section thoroughly before considering the use or products made of DuPont HYPALON synthetic rubber."

Since proper compounding *is* important, the mere inclusion of the word HYPALON in inflatable boat sales literature does not, in itself, justify the assumption that the product is of top quality. Some very poor boats appeared on the market which have broadcast the word HYPALON in their advertising literature.

Be alert also for sound-alike names like Hyperlon and Hydra-lon and check the literature where they appear to determine just what they are and whether they will meet your boating requirements.

The information below, the result of DuPont testing, is included to provide the reader with some insight into the properties which can make HYPALON an excellent inflatable boat ingredient.

PROPERTIES OF HYPALON

Weather Resistance: EXCELLENT. Sun, weather and ozone have virtually no effect on HYPALON's physical properties or its colors.

Colorability: EXCELLENT. Available in any color desired . . . pastels, whites, even translucent coatings. Colors are permanent, will not bleach or fade.

PROPERTIES OF HYPALON (Continued)

Thermal Properties: VERY GOOD. Coatings will perform satisfactorily from -50 degrees F to $+300$ degrees F.

Fluid Resistance: VERY GOOD. Performs well with oils, grease, gasoline, acids, and oxydizing chemicals.

Abrasion Resistance: EXCELLENT. Impartial scrub tests have demonstrated the outstanding abrasion resistance of HYPALON coated fabrics.

Fabrication, maintenance and repair: Fabric coatings based on HYPALON can be applied to all standard base fabrics (including the major synthetic fibers) using conventional processing techniques. It gives high coating adhesion, and is easy to clean and repair.

Flame Resistance: Fabric coatings based on HYPALON will not support combustion — are self-extinguishing when source of ignition is removed.

APPENDIX VI
Minimum Standards for Inflatable Boats

The following standard for inflatable boats was developed by the American Boat and Yacht Council, a non-profit organization composed of naval architects, marine engineers, marine underwriters, marine surveyors, manufacturers of small craft and their components, U.S. Coast Guard and consumers.

The standard is designed to provide guidance to boat builders and equipment manufacturers to insure the safety of the recreational boating public. These are minimum standards and compliance is voluntary, and in themselves they do not insure that a boat is a quality product. Nevertheless, they do establish important guidelines for the industry, and as the popularity of inflatable boating continues to grow the standard can provide a good basis for further, more exacting, requirements.

For additional information concerning these voluntary standards and recommended practices, or on other subjects relating to recreational boating or equipment, address inquiries to: ABYC, P.O. Box 806, Amityville, NY 11701.

241

INFLATABLE BOATS

PROJECT H—28 (ADOPTED AUGUST 30, 1976)   ABYC H—28—76

Based on ABYC's Assessment of the state of existing technology and the problems associated with achieving the requirements of this standard, ABYC recommends compliance with this standard by August 1, 1977.

H—28.1.   *PURPOSE*

These standards and practices are recommended as guides for load capacity, powering and materials for inflatable boats.

H—28.2.   *SCOPE*

These standards and recommended practices apply to all inflatable boats.

H—28.3.   *DEFINITIONS*

a.   *Inflatable Boat* — Any boat which achieves and maintains its intended shape and buoyancy through the medium of inflation.

b.   *Motor Mount* — A motor mounting means which does not significantly contribute to the boat's strength or shape.

c.   *Transom* — A rigid member necessary for the strength and shape of the boat and designed for mounting an outboard motor.

H—28.4.   *GENERAL*

a.   Capacity information shall be permanently displayed on the inflatable boat in a legible manner where it is clearly visible, showing:

(1)   Maximum horsepower. (See ABYC H—28.5.b., c. and d.)

(2)   Maximum weight capacity (persons, motor and gear) in pounds. (See ABYC H—28.5.a.(1).)

(3)   Maximum persons capacity in pounds. (See ABYC H—28.5.a.(2).)

NOTE: *Lesser values for the above capacities may be used at the manufacturer's option.*

b.   Instructions shall be provided by the manufacturer including the following information:

(1)   Safe operation.

(2)   Assembly and inflation instructions that will result in proper inflation of all chambers.

(3)   Repair instructions.

(4)   Recommended equipment.

c.   The recommended working pressure shall be permanently displayed on the inflatable boat in a readily visible location.

H–28.5.   *DESIGN AND CONSTRUCTION*

a.   *Load Capacity*

(1)   *Maximum Weight Capacity* – The maximum weight capacity marked on an inflatable boat must be a number that does not exceed three-quarters of the total volume of the main buoyancy-chambers in cubic feet times 62.4 less the boat weight in pounds.

L = .75D–W
L – Maximum Weight Capacity in pounds.
D – Total volume of Main Buoyancy–Chambers in cubic feet times 62.4, excluding removable chambers.
W – Weight of the boat hull, floorboards and all its permanent appurtenances in pounds. Outboard motors are not included.

NOTE: Compliance with certain state laws requires that the maximum capacity be .5D–W.

(2)   *Persons Capacity in Pounds* – The persons capacity shall not exceed the lesser of the values determined by the following formulas:

Persons Capacity (pounds) = (.75D–W) – (motor and gear weight if applicable)

Persons Capacity (pounds) = $\frac{Cockpit\ Area}{4} \times 150$

NOTE: Cockpit area is the area determined by the inside periphery at the centerline of the main chambers. This area shall not extend aft of the transom if the inflatable boat is so equipped.

WEIGHTS (POUNDS) OF OUTBOARD MOTOR
AND RELATED EQUIPMENT FOR VARIOUS BOAT HORSEPOWER RATINGS

Boat Horsepower Rating	Motor & Control Weight		Battery Weight		Full Portable Fuel Tank Weight
	Dry	Swamped	Dry	Submerged	
0 to 4	35	30	––	––	––
4.1 to 7	55	48	––	––	25
7.1 to 15	75	65	20	11	50
15.1 to 25	100	88	45	25	50
25.1 to 45	155	136	45	25	100
45.1 to 80	240	211	45	25	100
80.1 to 150	315	277	45	25	100
150.1 to 250	420	370	45	25	100
Transoms Designed For Twin Motors					
50.0 to 90	310	273	90	50	100
90.1 to 160	480	422	90	50	100
160.1 to 300	630	554	90	50	100
300.1 to 500	840	739	90	50	100

(H—28.5.)

b. *Powering for Inflatable Boats Equipped with a Motor Mount But No Transom*

The maximum horsepower marked on a boat shall not exceed the horsepower capacity determined as follows:

(1) Boats less than 9 feet (2.74 m) in length — 3 H.P. maximum.

(2) Boats from 9 feet to 12 feet (2.74 to 3.66 m) in length — 5 H.P. maximum.

(3) Boats 12 feet (3.66 m) in length and over — 7.5 H.P. maximum.

c. *Powering for Inflatable Boats with Transoms*

(1) The maximum horsepower marked on an inflatable boat with a transom shall not exceed the horsepower capacity determined as follows:

Factor = Boat Length (Feet) X Beam (Feet) (to nearest whole number).

Factor Range	Horsepower Formula
0—42	HP = 7.5
43—80	*HP = 10/9 X Factor — 40
Over 80	*HP = 1/2 X Factor + 10

*Horsepower may be rounded up to the next multiple of 5 unless the calculation results in an exact multiple of 5.

(2) *Remote Steering* — Inflatable boats rated for over 25 horsepower shall have provisions for installing remote steering in accordance with ABYC P—17, "Steering Systems".

d. *Confirmation of Powering Capacity*

Inflatable boat manufacturers should test and confirm the boat's ability to safely handle the recommended horsepower for which the boat is rated.

e. *Construction and Strength*

(1) *Compartmentation* — An inflatable boat shall be constructed so that there are two or more individual air compartments within the hull excluding detachable inflated chambers so that if one compartment becomes deflated the others will retain their integrity. The separate compartments shall conform to the following:

(a) Boats under 12.5 feet (3.81 m) in length, at least two separate compartments shall be provided.

(b) Boats 12.5 feet (3.81 m) in length or longer, at least three separate compartments shall be provided.

(c) The boat shall be capable of supporting 50 percent of the maximum weight capacity with the largest compartment deflated.

(2) *Pressure Retention* — When new, inflatable boats with all air compartments inflated to the manufacturer's suggested working gage pressures shall not lose more than 33 percent of this gage pressure over 24 hours of inflation. During the test period, appropriate corrections shall be made for changes in temperature and/or barometric pressure.

244

(H—28.5.e.)

(3) *Compartment Strength* — When new, each compartment shall withstand 1.5 times the manufacturer's suggested working gage pressure for 30 minutes with the adjacent compartments at atmospheric pressure. No evidence of failure shall occur.

(4) *Boat Strength* — When new, inflatable boats shall be able to withstand a pressure of 2½ times the manufacturer's suggested working gage pressure for ten minutes. No evidence of failure shall occur.

(5) *Transom and Motor Mount Strength* — The transom or motor mount and its attachment to the boat shall be designed to withstand the maximum stresses arising from:

   (a)   the forward and reverse thrust of the motor(s) representing the maximum horsepower capacity of the boat.

   (b)   the weight of such motor(s).

(6) *Compatability with the Marine Environment* — All materials used in the construction of an inflatable boat shall be resistant to exposure to salt water, fresh water, sunlight and motor fuels encountered during normal marine service.

Glossary

ACRILAN	Monsanto Company trademark for acrylic fiber which is highly resistant to deteriorating influences and dyes well. Frequently used in the manufacture of boat covers, etc.
ANTI-CAVITATION PLATE	A flanged horizontal plate located just above the propeller on outboard motors; designed to prevent the introduction of air to the whirling propeller.
ANTI-SPLASH VANES	On a sportboat, triangular pieces of fabric extending from the top of the transom, aft to the adjacent hull tubes, to minimize water splash from the engine.
ATHWARTSHIPS	Running from one side of the boat to the other.
BEACH GRADIENT	A measure of the slope of a beach.
BEAM	The width of the hull.
BECKETS	On inflatables a protruding, flattened, rubber or plastic device cemented to the hull for securing tie lines or loops such as those found on detachable bow dodgers, etc.
BOW DODGER	A fabric skirt or covering which spans the bow of the boat to protect equipment or passengers. Can be either fixed or removable.
BROACH	Turning broadside to the waves.
BULKHEAD	Nautical term for a partition. Dome or cone-shaped fabric bulkheads are used in inflatables to separate chambers.
CALENDERING	Passing fabric through very heavy opposing rollers to compress impregnating substances into the weave.

246.

CAVITATION — Overspeeding of the propeller due to the introduction of air into the water flow.

CHAMBERING — The separation of the hull tubes into several units to insure sufficient flotation in the event of puncture.

CUPPED PROPELLER — A propeller with a slight forward curvature on the leading edge to reduce cavitation.

"D" RINGS — Metal or plastic rings with one side flattened, which are cemented to the hull with fabric strips, and are used for attaching lines, snaps, etc. to the boat.

DACRON — DuPont trademark for polyester fiber.

DENIER — A term relating to the weight, in grams, of 9000 meters of individual thread. In itself denier is of no particular significance when comparing the strength of two different fabrics. To be of value the denier number must be multiplied by the thread count (the number of warp threads times the number of weft threads) in like-sized fabric samples. The higher the resulting figure, the stronger the fabric.

DINGHY — Small tender designed for use by yachtsmen and usually capable of mounting a small outboard motor.

DISPLACEMENT HULL — When not in motion a boat will displace its own weight in the water. Displacement hulls run at nearly the standing depth when moving. Compare with PLANING HULL.

DISPLACEMENT SPEED — The maximum speed which a boat with a displacement hull can achieve. Can be calculated in knots by taking the square root of the waterline length and multiplying by 1.25.

DOELFIN — A plastic fin with a cross-section shape resembling an aircraft wing which is clamped to the anti-cavitation plate of an outboard motor and aids the boat in its transition to a plane.

DOUBLERS — Fabric pieces inside the boat which serve to reinforce the joint between bottom and hull fabric. In boats with floorboards the doubler aids in reducing chafing damage between board edge and hull.

247

FIXED FLOOR BOARD	See THRUST BOARD.
FOLLOWING SEA	Waves coming at a boat from behind.
FREEBOARD	The amount of the boat that projects above the water.
HOGGING	The undesirable tendency of a boat to droop at both ends, forming a curve similar to a hog's back.
HOGGING STRIPS	Fabric reinforcing strips cemented along the tops of the hull tubes to counteract hogging in an inflatable boat.
HULL TUBE	The inflated tube forming the hull of an inflatable boat. Sometimes called a pontoon.
HYBRID BOAT	A boat with a fiberglass or other solid bottom, but with an inflated upper hull.
HYPALON	DuPont trade name for chlorosulfonated polyethylene, an extremely durable synthetic rubber made by reacting polyethylene with chlorine and sulphur. Used as a surface coating over neoprene rubber, or as a mixture with neoprene, to serve as a protecting and toughening agent.
INFLATABLE KEEL	A longitudinal tube placed between the floorboards and the fabric bottom of an inflatable boat to create a "V" shaped bottom.
"J" RIG	Large commercial riverboat formed by joining several long individual inflated tubes together.
JOINTED OARS	Oars which separate in the center for ease in stowing.
KEVLAR	DuPont tradename for a new, strong, and very light fiber beginning to be used in inflatable boat construction.
KNIFE COATING	A method of coating fabrics using a long blade to spread the impregnating substance on the material.
KNOT	A unit of speed equal to one nautical mile per hour.

LAMINATES	The multiple layers which form the fabric in inflatable boats.
LAPPED SEAM	A seam formed by overlapping one piece of fabric over another.
LAUNCHING WHEELS	Removable wheels which attach to the transom of a boat and permit it to be moved about on land.
LEEBOARDS	Adjustable boards located on the sides of some sailboats to help prevent sideways slip. The lee, or downwind board is forced down into the water while its opposite number is raised to reduce drag.
NAUTICAL MILE	6080 feet, or one minute of latitude.
NEOPRENE	A synthetic rubber often used to coat and airproof fabrics used in the manufacture of inflatable boats. More durable than natural rubber, but still susceptible to damage from the elements if left unprotected. Usually mixed or coated with Hypalon to increase its resistance.
NYLON	A polyamide fiber frequently used in the manufacture of inflatable boats which is immune to attack by mildew, moths, bacteria, dampness and other influences that rapidly deteriorate natural fibers.
OUTBOARD BRACKET	A detachable bracket used to mount an outboard motor on an inflatable dinghy. Also called MOTOR MOUNT.
OZONE	A variation of oxygen gas with a molecular formula of O_3. It is produced by the discharge of electricity in ordinary oxygen. Ozone is a much more powerful oxydizer than ordinary oxygen, and the cause of most aging in rubberized materials.
PILLOW SEAT	A pillow shaped inflated seat used for seating passengers in inflatable boats.
PFD	Personal Flotation Device. The U.S. Coast Guard requires that one of these be aboard your boat for each passenger.
PLANING HULL	A boat hull designed to ride up and on top of the

water when at cruising speed. Planing hulls offer much less resistance to the water and top speed depends on engine power.

PLANING SPEED
The minimum speed necessary to make a boat plane.

POLYESTER
A durable synthetic fiber with a low degree of stretch frequently used in coated form to manufacture inflatable boats. Produced under a variety of trade names such as DACRON, TREVIRA, TERYLENE.

POLY VINYL CHLORIDE
A thermoplastic resin used to airproof inflatable boat fabrics.

PONTOON
Alternate name for the hull tube. Also, in riverboating the term refers to the exceedingly large inflatable boats (22 feet and larger) used by commercial outfitters.

PORT
The left side of a boat when facing forward.

REGISTRATION NUMBERS
Numbers assigned by the government to identify individual boats. The number must be displayed when the boat is in use.

REINFORCED FABRIC
Fabric used in the construction of inflatable boats which has a fiber base, usually nylon or polyester.

RIP CURRENT
A fast current, moving seaward through the surf, and caused by the breakout of water trapped inside the surf line.

ROWING FRAME
A stout frame lashed to the top of the tubes on a riverboat to support the oars and the operator. Often includes a raised platform or netting for storage of equipment.

RUNNING LIGHTS
Night navigation lights.

SETS
The pattern of high and low waves caused by the interaction of wave patterns from two or more different storm centers.

SPORTBOAT
A high-speed inflatable boat designed to plane over

the water when powered by a large outboard motor.

SPORT DINGHY

Small sportboats capable of operating with or without floorboards, or with inflatable floors. Sometimes called Sport Tenders.

SPORT TENDER

See SPORT DINGHY.

SPRAY HOOD

Alternate name for BOW DODGER.

STARBOARD

The right side of the boat when facing forward.

STAYS

Wires or ropes used to support the mast of a sailboat.

STRINGER

Longitudinal member used to lock the floorboards together.

SURF ZONE

That strip of water along a beach where the surf is breaking.

THRUST BOARD

A fixed board, located in the forward part of sportboats equipped with inflatable keels, against which the remaining boards abut. Also called FIXED FLOORBOARD.

THWART SEAT

An inflated seat about the same diameter as the hull tubes which spans the interior of the boat.

TOWING BRIDLE

A "V" shaped bridle that attaches on either side of a boat's hull and fastens to the towing line by a sliding connector to permit the tow to oscillate while maintaining constant tension.

TOWING RINGS

Strong "D" rings located on either side of the bow of an inflatable boat for attaching a towing bridle.

TRANSOM

A flat wooden board spanning the hull tubes in the after section of the boat and designed to support the engine.

TUBE DIAMETER

The diameter of the hull tube. Larger diameter tubes increase buoyancy and add freeboard to the boat.

VALVE INSERT

A removable center plug found in some inflatable

boat valves to permit more rapid deflation of the hull.

WARP   A term designating the main or long cords in woven fabrics.

WEFT   A term designating the short or cross cords in woven fabrics.

WICKING   The passage of air along the threads of coated fabrics resulting in gradual loss of pressure in the boat.

Index

Illustrations are indicated in boldface type.

Index